A world full of dangerous threats and obstacles … a world many are covertly intrigued by, but never directly experience. Sandra has experienced a lifetime in the world of massage parlours, drugs, and sex. Not many of us on the 'other side' of that world become friends with people living that kind of life. It is hard to believe the gal I know today is the same one who lived the scary, unsettling experiences you will read about in the pages ahead.

— Dianne Snydal

In a world that often glosses over the depths of hardships, few have the courage to tell their story honestly. In this memoir, the reader will witness an extraordinary journey. A story of resilience, transformation, and the painful — but powerful — reclaiming of identity. Navigating an intense relationship with a narcissistic man, Sandra reveals the often-hidden reality of emotional and mental abuse. It is time for her story to be heard, I highly recommend this book.

— Lauren Casey, PhD

'We are all responsible for our own life's decisions.' This may be true, but as a young girl who was raped, pressured, and forced to become someone she didn't even recognise, did she really have a choice? For many years, she felt she didn't — until she made the decision to take back control.

— Amanda

Where The CHERRIES END UP

A MEMOIR

by

SANDRA RAMBERRAN

A Wood Dragon Book

Wood Dragon Books
Box 429, Mossbank, Saskatchewan, Canada S0H3B0

A Where the Cherries End Up - A Memoir

This memoir Is written using British spelling and punctuation.

ISBN: 978-1-990863-78-3 eBook
ISBN: 978-1-990863-77-6 Hardcover
ISBN: 978-1-990863-76-9 Paperback

Cover Design: Callum Jager, Hyperlight Artwork
Interior Design: Christine Lee

Published by: Wood Dragon Books
Post Office Box 429
Mossbank, Saskatchewan Canada S0H3G0
www.wooddragonbooks.com

To contact the publisher: wooddragonbooks@gmail.com
To contact the author: https://linktr.ee/Where.The.Cherries.End.Up

DEDICATION

I dedicate this memoir to my son.
I hope you understand that my life choices
were never about a lack of love for you,
but a lack of love for myself.

NOTE FROM THE AUTHOR

As my life unfolded in different directions, I have
felt a need to put pen to paper. What can happen to
attractive, young women, today as much as in my youth,
is unimaginable to people living peaceful lives in the
suburbs. Today, I am much older and, I hope, a great
deal wiser. It is my wish that my story be a small voice
of experience to the young women of today who may be
heading in the same, terrible, and regrettable direction.

This book is a memoir. It reflects my present recollections
of experiences over a period of years. Certain names and
identifying characteristics have been changed. Concealing
identities throughout the book may have given the book
an air of unreality — but to have identified exactly
where events took place and the people involved would
have meant a great deal of hurt for many innocent
people. It would also have been disrespectful of some
who have died - and an actual danger to others

1

IN THE BEGINNING

My life began in the small English village of Acomb, a quaint and quiet little place where everyone knew everyone else — along with much of everyone else's personal business.

I was the oldest girl of six children. My mother was devoted to us, especially to my youngest brother, who was born with a disability caused by a lack of oxygen to his brain during his delivery. His life was limited in its potential and he became the only one in the family who was not responsible for what he made of himself. My father was an alcoholic. I learned later in life how that happens. To his credit, my dad did his best with the tools, the knowledge, and the burdens that he had been given.

At a young age, I realised that boys were attracted to girls but, because of my naivety, I failed to understand why. Eventually, I learned that all boys were entranced, mesmerized, by the same thing — a girl who allowed them a kiss or whose knickers they could put their hands into.

One afternoon, when I was nine years old and in middle school, I ran home from recess and cried to Mam, 'Stuart Jones put his hands down my knickers!'

Back at the school in the headmistress's office, along with the boy in question, I learned something that stuck with me for life — it is both expected and accepted that a girl's body is not entirely her own. As a young girl in the headmistress's office, I had to point, show, and tell — which was embarrassing, to say the least. All that came of the incident was to be told, 'Boys will be boys.'

I am not sure what I had expected, but I remember thinking afterwards that maybe it had all been my own fault.

Not long after that school yard encounter, this lesson was underlined.

An older man used to trawl the lane for young, maturing schoolgirls and offer to put money in their training bras. We could keep what money he put there, but only if we allowed him to put the money in with his own hands. Many of us girls willingly went along with his little game so that we could get the cash to buy sweets or single cigarettes from the local shop. Initially we ran off, giggling, thinking the man rather stupid. It was not long, though, before I figured out that he was not stupid. He was a pervert and smart enough to take advantage of young girls. That experience reinforced just who was in control of my body — and it wasn't me.

Looking back, I certainly had a unique, on-the-street sex education. My girlfriends and I played outside from morning until night in the 1960s, often annoyed at having to go in even for something to eat. When we did go indoors, we would gulp down whatever was offered as fast as possible so we could go right back out again to play with our friends.

Of course, being out and about the neighbourhood offered time and opportunity to get into all kinds of trouble. Local boys and girls, generally being innocent rule breakers, hung out under lamp posts or sat against pub walls, cadging cigarettes while sharing chips from the local chippy.

In our last year of primary school, at the tender age of ten going on eleven, we were feeling very adult and all grown up. Five of us girls decided to run away from home. It would be exciting, not to mention fun. We went off into the local woods where we managed to build a fire. It soon turned dark. Then the rain came. We were all hungry and cold, and it wasn't long before we decided to go home. We promised ourselves to have another go at it at a later time ... when we could do it properly.

Our plan was to steal money from our parents and then go farther afield. My contribution came from my dad's pockets. Being drunk most days, he never knew what he had or didn't have in those pockets and likely would not miss what I removed.

With the theft of money complete, it wasn't long before the second bid for freedom was initiated. After school, we took a bus ride from our little village into the larger community of York. With our collective kitty, we purchased train tickets to the seaside town of Scarborough, an hour's train journey away. (We chose Scarborough because we were all very familiar with it — it was a favourite destination for many English folk.)

Stupidly, but with much excitement, we soon spent all our money on fair rides, fish and chips, candy floss, and cigs. We left the fairground with nothing but a hoard of trinkets that we had won at various gaming venues.

The night quickly turned cold and dark. We looked for a warm place to sleep. Initially, we thought the bus shelters or shop doorways would keep us from the bitter cold blowing in from the unforgiving North Sea. Eventually, we realised that to stay warm, we would have to get away from the oceanfront and make our way further into the town.

As we walked along the oceanfront, we noticed we were being followed by a police car. In fear of being asked where we got the money for the trinkets, we all agreed to throw the trinkets over the sea wall.

Sure enough, they did stop us, and asked where we lived and where we were going. It didn't take long for the truth to come out and the tears to flow. We were taken to the local police station where we were given ice cream while the officers called my Auntie Esme (who, unlike my parents, had both a phone and a car). Our return home was courtesy of my aunt who drove out to collect us. Upon reaching home, I was greeted at the door by my crying mother. Strangely, I was disappointed and angry that my dad was in bed with a belly full of beer — which I should have expected, but for some reason I did not.

'He doesn't care about me!' I screamed at Mam through my tears.

I know now that he did care, but because he had never received love himself while growing up, he couldn't possibly know how to give it to others.

My dad had come from a large family. No contraceptives in those days! His birth mother died during the birth of her last child (who also died). Her first seven children were fathered by a different man, who had died in the war. Growing up, the last three children (my father and his two sisters) felt resentment from their older step-siblings, probably due to the fact that my grandfather was known for his gambling and drinking and that my grandmother had make a very bad choice of a second husband.

After Grandma's death, it didn't take long for my grandad to depart with his brood of three, leaving the older children to look after themselves with the help of their father's relatives.

With his three children in tow, he went to relatives for help and a place to sleep. As they approached one of their relative's homes, they were told not to cross the front step because it had just been scrubbed with soap and water. 'Sorry, we can't help,' one of the relatives called from inside the house, adding, 'Here's a banana,' which was tossed across the threshold. My aunt, Hilda, the eldest of the three siblings, recalls the family of four huddling together, trying to sleep in fields and telephone kiosks. Her most vivid memory was of my father crying nonstop with hunger.

Eventually, due to the family's homeless state, the authorities were alerted and they took the girls, aged six and seven, and placed them in the Dr. Barnado's Home for Children. It was decided by social services that Grandad could keep his five-year-old son because by then Grandad was in the process of moving in with a woman, who we all came to know as Grandma Tilly. Dad told us stories of the many beatings he suffered at Grandma Tilly's hands. When he was sent to school with no breakfast, he was told by Tilly not to say anything of his hunger otherwise he would be taken to Dr. Barnado's, just like his sisters.

Yet, as is still the case, many people somehow survive and grow in spite of the odds against them, though they may well be damaged in the process. That's how it was for both of my parents. They met, fell in love, tied the knot, and survived to pass their seed on to the next generation.

Although we only met my grandfather once, my two sisters and I all share the same memory. Grandad had lost a limb in the war and had a wooden leg. To entertain us, he would pull out from the draw a stuffed bird that looked like a cute, little robin red breast. He would wind up the toy, let it go, and it chirped across the velvet tablecloth.

But there is a reason they say, 'The fruit doesn't fall far from the tree.' My dad was no exception to the rule. He followed in his father's footsteps regarding his bad habits of drinking and gambling.

My mam was a strong-willed person, which probably helped her survive. Just putting food on the table was a challenge. In the constant struggle, she worked very hard, taking part-time jobs when she could get them. Our home was not one of laughter or good times and it was very evident to me that Mum and Dad were no longer in love.

My two older brothers, senior to me by a five-year and a four-year gap, were rarely home. When they were, they were rough on us girls. When my mum went out to work, I babysat my two younger sisters and my younger brother. I don't remember my eldest brother being at home — he was habitually out. My other older brother would always punch me on his way out the door.

I would yell, 'What was that for?'

He would yell back, 'Because I don't like you!' As a teenager, he was just damn mean.

Now adults, my brothers are more respectful and the violence of our youth has faded into history. It is shocking to me that now, in our later years, we are so very close. Just as shocking is the fact that we never speak of my brother's early physical violence towards me. (My sisters and I didn't always get along, but it only ever escalated to harsh words.)

Dad never lifted a finger at home to help in any way. He was a seasonal worker, the so-called 'bread winner' and expected his dinner to be on the table when he got home. My dad was always well dressed when he wasn't at work — *fussy about his appearance* would be an understatement. He was a real *ladies' man,* as they used to say. A handsome man admired for his good looks and blond curls — but sadly also renowned for his short temper. He liked his shoes to be shined in readiness for when he might want to go out again. He would often pay money to whoever did the job, which was usually me — after all, I was the oldest girl. (The significance of shiny shoes impacted me. As an adult, I have always been impressed with men who take the time to shine their shoes.)

Mam was a soft spoken, beautiful woman. She was an introvert and even as she was busy caring for us children, washing, cooking, and cleaning, she was very quiet about it. In later years, when life became easier for her, she kept secret those stories of the hard days gone by. It was only through our asking and talking to other family members did we learn details about her upbringing.

Her mum died of a brain tumour when Mam was only three years old and her father quickly remarried. I was told that Mam's father was a very strict man and because of his behaviour, my mum held a bitterness towards him. Mum's sister, Esme, was five years older than Mum. The two sisters couldn't have been more different; Esme was a chatterbox, interested in everyone's business, while my mum was always very quiet. Their new stepmom had an affinity towards Esme, but not towards Mum, and life became more and more difficult for my mother in the new household.

When mam was only nine years old, her father was knocked off his bicycle by an army lorry and killed instantly. She had been unhappy living with her father and his new wife and now that her father was no longer alive, she made the choice to leave. She was accepted with open arms at her Auntie Flo's house.

As the six of us grew up, we all knew that Mum loved us, not because she told us so, but because she showed us in many ways. She only spoke the words, 'I love you' to me once, and that was late in her life when she was terminally ill.

We were poor growing up in the 1950s; we just didn't realise it. We had better days when Dad was working at his seasonal job; the influx of money was very noticeable. When Dad was out of work, we received free school lunches and government support in the form of vouchers. The government coupons were used to buy our school uniforms, which were a mandatory shirt and tie — even for the girls.

I don't remember one single day when Dad did not go to the pub. Whilst he was not working, he went twice a day. He would come home for dinner and then go back out afterwards. He would never nap in the chair, there were too many of us kids making noise — he always went to his bedroom for a proper sleep. When he wasn't working, his daily life was a cycle of pub, dinner, nap, pub, sleep — seven days a week. That was all he seemed to care about.

Many a day when dad was taking his afternoon nap, I would creep on my hands and knees around the edge of his bed, listening to the rhythm of his snoring before stealing a couple of cigs from his night table. I was always in fear of him waking but obviously I wanted a cigarette badly enough that I was willing to take the risk. My dad never raised a hand to us girls. He didn't have to; he would raise his voice and that was enough.

Mum would book me off every Friday from school lunch and give me money for fish and chips. Unbeknownst to her, I would buy only a small bag of chips, leaving enough money for a packet of five cigarettes. I was clearly getting more and more addicted to smoking as any spare money I could get my hands on went to this habit. The local shop had machines outside on the wall that sold cigarettes in packets of five, making it easy to avoid any underage smoking rule. It was cool to smoke back then. All the advertising on television told you so. In his heyday, my dad smoked sixty cigarettes a day and drank as many as fifteen pints of beer daily. (Mum never drank and never smoked.)

Every summer, Mum, my sisters, my youngest brother, and I went on a one-day trip. We always spoke of it as 'our holiday.' (Dad and my two eldest brothers never joined us.) Organized by Dad's local pub, we would take a one-hour coach ride to the nearest seaside location. It was a time filled with the fun of running in and out of the sea, building sandcastles on the beach, and eating a lunch of Mum's delicious homemade egg salad sandwiches. We would take donkey rides up and down the beach and then enjoy a treat of a large ice cream with chocolate flake. (In our adult years, if we three were all together in the same country, we would go back there and repeat as many of these special moments of our childhood.)

Other children at school used to come back after the summer school break and speak of taking holidays abroad to warmer climates, telling stories of hotels and swimming pools. Then, there were the children with families that booked caravans and stayed for a month at a time at the many seaside resorts up and down the coastline. Still, we enjoyed our one-day out — we were not the only family that never went on holiday for a longer period of time.

As young as we were, we knew that money was never in abundance. At Christmastime, we knew better than to have a 'wish list' of items like other children. We happily received chocolate bars and fruit and simple toys like marbles, skipping ropes, or colouring books. Mam always baked and whatever we smelled baking in the kitchen was looked forward to with as much anticipation as our small gifts.

In later years, Mam often said that out of all six children, I gave her the most trouble. I wasn't surprised to hear that. I loved my mum dearly, but looking back — I realise that I did give her reason to worry.

Her focus was ensuring that Dad never had a reason to become upset. For example, my father would regularly come home in the evening with his belly full of beer and ask, 'Kids. They all in bed?'

Even if I was still out of the house, my mum would answer, 'Yes.'

Dad would then turn the key to lock the door.

Once Dad had fallen asleep, Mum would get up and wait for me. From outside, I would see the front curtain move to one side and I knew that it was my mam waiting for me to come home. She would open the door and whisper, 'Quiet. Upstairs. Go. Your dad thinks you are already in bed.'

I felt that my mum covered up a lot of my misbehaviours to keep peace with Dad. I never feared my father, I remember him being a fun drunk. I also felt that I was his favourite child — but I am sure my sisters each felt the same way.

His demeanour towards my brothers was very different. One time, Dad knocked out my eldest brother's front tooth for supposedly taking a bike that belonged to my brother's friend without permission.

Even our neighbour was in fear of Dad and would hold back from complaining about us children hopping the fence and stealing his apples. My dad had a very short temper and I understand more today why Mam hid our mischievousness from him on a regular basis.

I was often scolded at school. It seemed I was always in trouble. I was sent home many times to wash the makeup off my face. Other infractions included not wearing my school tie, wearing my skirt too short, and smoking in the playground. When I was caught misbehaving, I got the 'slipper.' That meant I had to take off my shoe and give it to the teacher, and then bend over so she could whack me on the butt with the shoe in front of the class. ('Bad' boys were sent to the headmaster's office where they had to hold out an open-palmed hand so that the headmaster could come down with the cane across the fingertips.)

I hated school and could not wait to leave it for good. I got a job delivering the local newspaper, but soon decided that early cold mornings were not for me. I went carol singing at Christmas time which gave me pocket money for gifts. (One year, my friends and I donated the money to my youngest brother's school. It was a special school for children with learning difficulties. The idea for the donation was my mum's but I thought it was a great thing to do as well. My brother has always been an adored sibling in our family. I know Mum and Dad were very proud when we took the donation to the school.)

Whilst in my last year of school, I applied for a part-time job at a news agents in the centre of York. I worked the Saturday shift and had an hour off for lunch. I loved it. I felt good about it … all grown up. I had responsibility and most of all, at long last,

I had my own money. It made me feel I was done with childhood.

I also soon realised that when girls are done with childhood games, they start to chase boys. Then, of course, the boys chase them right back. Chasing boys and being chased soon became my full-time focus. It was fun. Boys were fun and, best of all, they liked me.

2

RAPE

Barely into my teens, I discovered that boys were not always so much fun.

My school friend, Laurel, and I spent a lot of time riding the local bus. We never paid for a ticket, mostly due to the reason that the conductor was smitten with Laurel — just as she was with him. Unlike the bus driver who sat in his own compartment at the front of the bus, the conductor collected fares, a job which allowed considerable time for chatting and flirting; we had such fun, joking and laughing with him.

The bus reached the terminal where the driver and conductor had a break before making their return journey back into town. This final stop was near the driver's home. Laurel and I got off the bus and followed them both into the driver's house. I was busting to go to the loo, which was at the top of the stairs on the second floor.

After taking care of that personal urgency, I opened the door of the loo to find the bus driver standing there. Immediately, he grabbed me and tried to kiss me. Not at first realizing what was happening, I protested with a mere giggle, then an obvious show of unwillingness.

The next thing I knew, I was being manoeuvred into the nearest bedroom. Then, he was on top of me, and his hands were all over me. When I raised my voice a little, his large hand moved quickly to cover my mouth.

'You know you like it,' he said, along with other words designed to convince me to stop struggling and start co-operating.

At 13 years old, I did not fully understand what happened that day, but soon after I discovered the words for what he had done. He had *raped* me and taken my virginity.

I will never forget that man, nor his name. He had hurt me, made me bleed.

For the longest time after, I believed it had all been my fault. If I hadn't been so naïve and scared, I would have told an adult. When I take my mind back to that day, it's like a fresh memory. It is still very hurtful to know that he got away with doing that to me.

I didn't tell Laurel. I didn't cry. I went silent. When I reached home, I told my younger sister, but I don't think she understood the seriousness of it all. But frivolously riding on the buses ended immediately.

Many years later, I bumped into the conductor. Wondering if he remembered me or, more to the point, knew what his colleague had done to me, I asked him. He looked gob-smacked. He said he didn't know anything about what had happened. I didn't believe him.

3

YOUNG LOVE

A year after the sexual assault, I was spending many of my evenings at the recreation ground known to the locals as *The Green*. A lot of the older boys hung out there, showing off their motorbikes. One of them was Barry, who I found to be very handsome. He was several years older than me. Bolstered by his tales of his burglary exploits and prison sentences, he had a magnetic, bad boy personality. He flirted with most of the girls in my circle of friends. His motorbike had a sidecar and he often took girls for a spin.

I was nearing fifteen when Barry picked me out of the group. He took me on a real date to my first pub, bought me drinks, and kissed me. I thought we were dating. He made me feel special.

He was covered in tattoos. He not only had them on himself, but he had the tools and the know-how to tattoo other people. I was one of his practice canvases. After much encouragement from Barry, I agreed to a discreet tattoo on my stomach of a beautiful butterfly entwined with a sparrow on a flowering branch. As this was a permanent tattoo, I chose a location where I knew my mum would never see it.

Barry and I would meet up most days. He was the first person that I wanted to have sex with, but he never seemed to be interested in anything other than kissing.

One day, Barry was arrested by the police and taken to the station for questioning. He was charged with burglary. He was convicted and sentenced to a prison term of two years. During his time of incarceration, I would take the bus out to visit him. I also wrote love letters to him and received replies via an older friend's address. I hid his correspondence from my parents.

In the summer of 1969, two weeks short of my fifteenth birthday, I finished school for good. I had no interest in the technical college courses that were required to obtain a skilled job. I was determined to find full-time work — and did so at a busy department store in the centre of York. I loved my new job at the haberdashery counter, selling all kinds of sewing things. With my first wage, I bought Mum a present — a sewing basket complete with contents. She adored it and used it often.

In those days, the girls I knew belonged to different groups, but not 'gangs' as they are known today. They were just different groups of girls who made a name for themselves by acting tough or unique. Some girls were tougher than others, apt to give you a good kicking just for staring at them in a way that they felt was rude. One such girl scared the hell out of me. She was five years my senior. Out of fear of her, I would give her things over the haberdashery counter without charging her. I would put just one penny into the till and then pretend to give her change. Over time, she bought different items, such as scissors, cottons, and threads.

One day, I met Alfie — a man several years older than me and of a similar age to Barry. He was very handsome and reminded me of my father.

When I turned sixteen, he bought me an Elvis record set. He told me that he loved me. We spent many hours together, and when we couldn't be together, we made arrangements to talk from the local phone booths. Alfie had a big motorcycle and I thought he looked sexy in all his leather attire. We would often ride out to public parks, and find a cozy corner to kiss and cuddle. When we were able to get the use of a bed, courtesy of one of his friends, we made love. I thought it was 'proper' love making because he taught me many things. During our relationship, he introduced me to oral sex, and other 'things' that I had only previously read about.

Through gossip, I found out that Alfie had a wife and son. This was surprising as he had never mentioned his married-with-family status to me. Alfie was very forward with his words of love and certainly acted like he was a single man. In my naivety, I thought that if he was not concerned about his wife finding out about his cheating, then neither should I be.

One day after leaving work, my sister met me at the bus stop and told me that Alfie's wife had been to our house and had spoken to Mam. My sister felt I should be prepared. Mam was upset with me, to put it mildly. Alfie's wife had told her I was having an affair with her husband and, furthermore, it was ongoing, and she had found condoms in his pocket. Hence Mam's distress!

The only time my mother ever hit me was when I arrived home that day. She slapped me from the kitchen all the way down the hallway and into the lounge where I curled up in a ball on the settee to protect myself.

Obviously, my mum was extremely disappointed and angry with me, but the only thought that went through my mind had nothing to do with the fact that Alfie's wife had arrived at the door. I was focused on the fact that his wife had found condoms! That was a surprise to me. Alfie had never used a condom when he was with me, so who did he use them with? Who else was the man I thought I loved seeing?

Mam never told Dad about my dalliance with Alfie and certainly nothing about the wife's visit. Alfie and I stopped seeing each other. Life went on.

When Barry had served his time in prison, we resumed our romance.

Eventually, Alfie discovered that, while we had been together, I had also been visiting Barry in prison. Whenever I bumped into Alfie, he would try to intimidate me by calling me names. If I saw him when I went into town, I would duck in and out of shop doorways to avoid him. When we were within earshot of each other, he would shout at me and screw up his face in disgust.

'How's Barry?' he would say sarcastically.

One night, Barry and I bumped into Alfie in a bar in town. Alfie must have thought he had a reason to fight Barry due to the two-timing. Soon the two men were pushing and shoving each other, and it wasn't long before a fist fight began. Alfie got the better of Barry and left him on the ground. I helped Barry get up and we walked home, mostly in silence.

A few days passed and Barry was picked up and taken back to prison. He had not checked in with his parole officer as he had been instructed.

My working life at the department store continued. Every other day, my manager put me on the cigarette kiosk. I loved that because I could see outside through the large, plate glass windows. When friends and family came into town shopping, they would always stop by to say hello.

Unfortunately, my job at the store was short-lived. I was only there for a year before I was caught giving cheaper-than-cheap items to my 'bully' friend and I was fired. I was charged with theft and was required to appear in court to answer for my wrong doings. Luckily, I got off with a one-year conditional discharge. This meant that if I stayed out of trouble for the next twelve months, the courts wouldn't impose a fine or send me to

jail. This sentence given by the judge was a slap on the wrist —
likely due to my age and the fact that my devoted Mum came
with me to court. Still, it was all a very harrowing experience. I
had just turned sixteen years of age.

Having failed miserably in customer service, I looked
for and found work in factories. I worked in a paper factory
for a month but I didn't like it so I quit. Then, I was hired on
at a chicken factory where my role was to cut a hole in the
chicken's bottom. My task was to pull out the poop bags as they
passed by on a line hung from the ceiling. The chickens were
passing at a good speed so there was no time to joke around
with other workers — including the girl next to me who was
an old school friend.

I stabbed one chicken and as I pulled out the poop bag,
it burst, the contents spurting out onto my friend's face. I turned
to look at her and the mess I had caused. We were both laughing
so hard, we had to step away from the line, leaving chickens
to sail by uncut.

Girls further down the line were shouting, 'Who's not
cutting? What are you doing up there? For fuck's sake, stop the
belt! Stop the chickens!'

By now my friend and I were leaning against the back
wall, our laughter turned into hysterics.

Needless to say, we both were fired.

It didn't take me long to find other work and soon
I was settled into a job at the renowned chocolate factory,
Joseph Terry and Sons.

I loved my new job. I was put to work in the packing
department. My job entailed using a small, handheld iron similar

in shape to a lollipop. This was used to heat the cellophane on all sizes and shapes of boxes of chocolates. I prided myself on being the fastest of the workers on our table of four. With my first wages, I bought a bicycle so I could ride the four miles to and from work as opposed to taking the bus.

Eventually, I was promoted to Machine Operator and put in charge of our team. I never missed a day of work and always took overtime when it was offered. I loved the girls that I was teamed up with. We would sometimes sing along with the loud radio that played overhead. We worked on piece work and I would encourage the girls to go faster so that we could get our crate loads of chocolates finished sooner. We got paid as a team so the more we did, the more money we could all make.

4

TOUGH WOMEN

One evening, my old school-friend, Linda, and I went out to a popular bar called *Tramways*. It always had a good payout for its Bingo sessions and had live local bands and dancing. We played bingo for a while and were having a quiet night — until a girl got up from her table of friends and came toward us, an angry look on her face. She came right up to us and immediately started accusing Linda of having a fling with her boyfriend.

The accuser was backed up by her entourage. Within seconds, I made the decision to purposely upturn the table of drinks to prevent Linda or me from being punched in the face. Instantly, the voices and threats became louder. Our drinks spilled onto our aggressors, soaking them with beer. This really pissed them off.

Linda and I were not fighters — we needed to get out of there as fast as we could before we took a beating. We made our way towards the revolving front door as quickly as we could. In the confusion that reigned in the escape attempt, I unintentionally trapped a girl's head in the turnstile. I dared not let go for fear of the lot of them immediately, and violently, pouncing on us.

Finally, the club steward came to see what all the commotion was about. He quickly realised the girls on the inside of the club were angry and, clearly, after the two of us. He took over my hold on the door and told us to run. We did not need to be told twice. We were gone in an instant!

Down the street in the quiet of the night, I heard someone shouting, 'You dare show your face in town again and I will get you!'

It was the girl whose head I had clamped in the door. I later found out, to my horror, she was a person who had a reputation for cutting people with broken beer glasses.

I stayed out of York's city centre for some time. Eventually, I decided to send word to the girl whose head I had accidentally trapped in the revolving door. I felt it was important for me to try to resolve the conflict as she was sending and making threats via her friends, warning me not to go into town. I wanted to explain that it wasn't my fault that the fight erupted and I was truly sorry about how it had all unfolded.

I waited in the toilets of the pre-arranged meeting place. It was a well-known bar called *The Tavern In The Town*. I knew exactly what I was going to say when she walked in. I was going to explain that I had just been an onlooker and that

I was truly sorry that her head got caught in the turnstile. But, as soon as she walked in, with an entourage to support her, I knew I was in trouble.

She stepped up to me with her hands together in a double fist and gave me a swift upper cut under the chin, followed immediately with a kick to my shins. I fell to the floor and took more kicks while her audience of friends laughed with approval and delight.

After what seemed like the slowest few minutes of my life, they all left. I pulled myself up into a standing position and leaned on the sink, looking in the mirror to check out the damage to my face. I went home hurting in places that I never knew I had.

My experience with that crazed woman was not over. A few weeks after the washroom brawl, I went into town with Lorraine, a woman for whom I used to babysit. She was ten years my senior. In the first pub we went to, Lorraine stepped up to the bar to order drinks while I stood back waiting.

She started chatting to the girl beside her. As the stranger turned her face towards me, I froze on the spot. Lorraine was making general and polite conversation with none other than the girl that had given me a beating a few weeks earlier! The bar was busy, standing room only, which was common for a weekend pub crawl. When Lorraine moved away from the bar with our drinks, the crowd swallowed up my attacker, blocking us from her view. Lorraine passed me my drink and I said, 'Drink up fast. It's too busy in here. Let's go somewhere else.'

Once we had finished our drinks, and stepped outside the pub door, I told Lorraine who it was that she had been talking to at the bar. I explained that she was the one who had beaten me up in the toilets at The Tavern In The Town. It turned out that Lorraine knew my attacker — they had gone to the same school.

'I'm not scared of her,' Lorraine said, turning to go back into the pub to either talk or fight it out. Thankfully, I convinced her to leave the place.

We went in and out of several bars and soon the evening passed and it was time to head home. At the taxi rank, my heart dropped to the ground. There she was! The crazed one, waiting in line for a taxi. She looked over as we joined the queue and then began to approach us.

Lorraine stood in front of me and said, 'If you are going to hit her again, you will have to hit me first.' I knew with a head full of beer on both sides, the situation was going to get messy.

The thumping and kicking started. A taxi driver helped to separate them whilst I cowardly moved out of the way. I jumped into his cab and held the door open for Lorraine. I shouted from the back seat, 'Lorraine! Get in the taxi! Hurry!' I am pretty sure Lorraine came worse off in that scuffle, not only because she had too much to drink, but also because she was wearing a large cowl neck sweater and the attacker had pulled it over her head, covering Lorraine's eyes so she couldn't see where her punches were landing. The taxi driver was very helpful in separating the two of them and we were soon on our way home.

I was thankful that I never bumped into the woman again.

5

DEEPLY IN LOVE

After the beating, it took me some time to feel truly confident going out into town. I started to go out with friends to a newly opened nightclub that was quite different from the pubs we generally frequented.

To my surprise, the popular tough-guy leather jackets were not even allowed. Instead, men were dressed to impress, and one of them did just that. He walked into my life wearing a three-piece suit and tie. I thought he was handsome, to say the least.

We introduced ourselves. He told me his name was Richard. Conversation flowed easily and soon he was telling me that he was legally separated with three small children. He went on to say that he was presently staying at his parents' home until things were legalised.

Richard and I talked through the evening about anything

and everything. The atmosphere was electric; between the music and the many drinks that flowed, it was a perfect setting for falling for the man of your dreams. I hung on to everything he said. I loved his big blue eyes and how his hair was quiffed into a wave. I loved his laugh and, most of all, I loved the way he kissed me. It was easy to get carried away in the moment and I knew that Richard was feeling the same.

Later, in the early hours after we left the club, he took me to see his workshop where he and his partner did the joinery work for all the jobs that Richard brought in.

We made love in the workshop. It was passionate and rushed — as if we would run out of time if we didn't get each other's clothes off quickly. (Later, I made him swear he would never speak of the Bridgette Jones girdle I was wearing even though I was just all of nine stone soaking wet - 126 pounds. I thought I was overweight. What a joke ... a true sign of my insecurity.)

After that first night, we became inseparable and I felt that he loved me as much as I loved him.

Of course, I never talked about Barry, whom I had visited in prison and continued to write to. But when Richard told me his divorce papers had come through, I decided it was time to send Barry a 'Dear John' letter. I had fallen head over heels for Richard.

Upon hearing of my new 'love liaison,' Barry sent instructions to one of his tough cronies on the outside to beat up Richard. This particular crony was dating my friend, Linda, and as soon as she heard about the request coming from Barry in prison, she didn't hesitate in telling me about the request.

Linda and I convinced her boyfriend that my relationship with Richard was not a fly-by-night thing, that we were truly in love and talking wedding bells, so he decided not to confront Richard.

Richard had no idea about Barry's instructions for an assault against him. Richard lived in a different world with a completely different circle of friends. He owned his own business and wore business attire — shirts, ties, and jackets. Barry's world was all 'Teddy Boys,' consisting of motorcycles, leather jackets, 'bopper shoes,' velvet trimmed jackets, and coifed Elvis Presley hair styles.

One night, Richard and I ended up in a nightclub that I was not familiar with. When I saw Alfie there with a bunch of his biker friends, I immediately felt uncomfortable. I also noticed Linda's boyfriend standing at the bar.

Richard told me he was going to the washroom. After half an hour, I went to look for him. When the men's washroom door opened, I saw Richard struggling to stand up from the floor. He had pulled his handkerchief from his pocket and was holding it to his cheek. Someone had given him a punch to the face. He quickly regained his stance, saw me waiting, and said, 'Let's go.'

I kept quiet about my theories as to who punched Richard. I hadn't told him anything about my past boyfriends — I didn't want to take the risk that he would leave me.

I loved Richard but he certainly was not perfect. He gave me a 'dose,' which is how people referred to venereal disease in those days. I was convinced it was him as I had been sexually faithful to him and therefore it simply could not have come from anyone else.

Against all doctors' orders and warnings to abstain

from sexual activity and alcohol while taking medication, we continued to drink and have sex whenever the opportunity arose. Hence, because we never listened to our doctor, the medical problem worsened. We were on repeat medication and stronger instructions to abstain from having sex.

Soon after the resolution of our health problem, we began talking about breaking up. I knew he did not contract the venereal disease from me, so I told him emphatically that if our relationship was to continue, we had to be honest with each other. Richard claimed he had been given 'the gift' by a woman he had picked up in York prior to our getting so serious about one another. I knew that I loved him, so I decided to forgive him and let the issue drop.

Not long after the infections were over and life got back to normalcy, he asked me to marry him. I had just turned eighteen so he told me I needed to be sure of my answer because I was much younger than he was. He said he knew what he wanted but that I had to be sure it was what I wanted as well. By this time, his divorce had been finalized and his wife had been given full custody of the children.

I decided that marrying Richard *was* what I wanted and, from that moment on, all I had to do was to pick out my wedding dress and choose my bridesmaids. Not once did I have to worry about the cost. Richard took care of everything.

Mam asked, 'Why do you have to pick such an expensive engagement ring? You could use that money to get settled.'

In retrospect, it was indeed quite a large sum, but Richard and I had both fallen in love with my choice of a diamond ring, one that would match our two gold wedding bands.

While we were in the midst of wedding planning, my father's sisters and their husbands were in England visiting from Canada. They had all emigrated years earlier. One of my uncles talked about how great the country was and how he would sponsor us if we wanted to emigrate after we were married. Richard was instantly on board and it didn't take much to convince me that this was a fantastic idea.

Richard took care of all the bookings for the church, the reception, and the wedding photographer, as well as our passports and the paperwork for our journey to Canada.

We had a lovely church wedding. I had four bridesmaids – Richard's two younger sisters and my two younger sisters. My dress was beautiful and I truly felt like a princess. Leaving my job at the chocolate factory was tearful. I had worked there for over three years and made some very close friends, many who came to the wedding. My life was unfolding so beautifully it was hard for me to believe that I could be so happy after all the bullshit that I had experienced so far in my life.

I truly, truly loved Richard. He had such a charismatic personality. I used to laugh just at his laugh. It was such a hearty, belly laugh. He had a reputation for being a bit of a conman (similar to the reputation my dad had acquired), mostly because he didn't pay his bills, or at least not on time, making people wait a long time to collect the monies owed to them. He was a daring and gloating games player — poker, snooker, darts — he always wanted to wage money. People often said, 'If Richard fell into a pile of shit, he would come up smelling of roses.'

I found the banter back and forth exciting. Richard had those 'man about town' traits that my father had, but untainted by excessive drinking. Richard never used to drink very much. Some nights when we went out, one pint would last him an hour or more. He got along especially well with my dad and they would often play snooker together. I used to love watching and listening to them both; they took great pleasure in winding each other up in a fun way.

Richard loved his parents and family as much as I loved my own, hence it was a very upsetting scene at the airport when we left England. Saying goodbye was one of the hardest things to do for both of us. Many tears flowed that day.

We were married on a Saturday. The following Monday, we flew to territory unknown — to a place where we had heard the weather could be brutally cold in the winter, reaching temperatures of -40C, and with equally brutal summers with temperatures of 30C and higher. But having just turned 19, having never been on a jet plane, my naïve self was not frightened by the prospect ... just somewhat nervous and extremely excited.

Within a few weeks, Richard had a job in the bank where my uncle was the manager. The new income enabled us to move out of my uncle's home and into a small, one-bedroom apartment. I was hired on at the local children's hospital and it seemed our future was very bright.

Before long, Richard decided banking was not for him. After trying a few different types of jobs, he felt he had to work for himself. He did just that and, not unexpectedly, with a great deal of success. He bought a truck and advertised his new construction company. He decided roofing would be his specialty. Before long, he had purchased another truck, hired several men, and business boomed.

I was never involved in any of the business, property, or financial decisions. I trusted easily in those days and trusted Richard implicitly. To me, we were an ideal couple. I was so happy and so in love that I waited on him hand and foot. Whenever possible, I would try to have his bath pulled and dinner on the table when he came home. The business was growing fast due to the advertising Richard placed. Most evenings, we would go out together until dark, responding to the need for free estimates.

My job at the hospital was gratifying. I was known as the 'treat' lady. Every afternoon, I would fill my trolley with jelly, ice cream, and juices, and then, much to the delight of the young patients, make the rounds. They often greeted me with shouts of 'Hooray! The treat lady is here!'

Within a couple of years, Richard had bought and sold three or four different homes. He was always looking for good deals which enabled us to climb the property ladder. He eventually purchased a three-story house that was large enough to accommodate friends and family alike. I called this my *forever home* as it was where most of my beautiful memories were created, the home that we lived in together for the longest period of time. It was separated into individual apartments. With three stories, there was enough room for anyone that wanted to visit or rent.

We travelled back to England for the holidays. En route home, for my 21st birthday, Richard bought tickets to Elvis

Presley's show in Las Vegas. Sometimes, I couldn't help but daydream — how lucky I was, coming from a tiny village in the north of England and now experiencing such an exciting event.

We went back to England as often as we could. We often took skiing trips to a place called Sugar Hills which was located not far from where we lived and just over the American border. (Most of our trips were in the winter because that was the slow season for Richard's business.)

Eventually, I left my job at the hospital to become a stay-at-home secretary for the ever-growing business. It didn't take long after Richard's purchase of our dream home, to fill it with friends and visiting family. During one visit, Richard's brother and my brother decided to stay in our adopted country and apply for landed-immigrant status. In time, my sister, her husband, and their two-year-old daughter decided to do the same thing. Our respective parents also came to visit for long holidays, along with other family members. At the time, I thought it was all some kind of dream life we were living.

In due course, Richard bought yet another three-story house on the same street as our dream home. It was separated into individual apartments which made it easier for Richard to rent out the units to people who worked for him. Money was plentiful, life was good, and it kept getting better. I never had to worry about finances or anything related to bills. Richard took care of everything. Every week, he put cash in my hand and I walked over to the grocery store. He said he was always in awe of how I could come back home with no change!

After I quit working at the hospital, we decided to try to have a baby. I monitored my body temperature for ovulation and did everything that the doctor suggested. However, after several tests, it was discovered that my fallopian tubes were very scarred and therefore blocked, and chances of pregnancy were slim to nil.

Clearly, the doctors at the VD clinic back in England had been right when they advised me that the disease could sometimes cause infertility. I kept the news of my doctor's diagnosis from Richard, never explaining that there was a problem. I did not want him to feel responsible, so I just told him the doctor had said, 'Keep trying. It will happen.'

We still went back to England for an annual winter holiday when possible. On our earliest trips to England, Richard and I always went out together in the evenings. As time went on, Richard occasionally went out without me, but soon, spending his evenings with 'the boys' becoming a regular thing. With that, the wonderful mirage of the perfect life and marriage began to fade, replaced by a much uglier thing called *mistrust*. I asked myself, 'Why does he all of a sudden want to be out with the boys instead of spending time with me?'

One evening, he came home late. He said, 'I am going back out. I will be home around three, or four.'

'In the morning?'

'I'm going shooting.'

'I don't believe you.'

'Come along if you like. It's just a bunch of men shooting rabbits.'

So, I went along. He was excited to use the new 22-calibre rifle he had brought with him from Canada. He had packed it into his suitcase along with his clothes, which I thought would be a problem if he was caught with it in his luggage.

So, we set off to shoot rabbits — Richard with his new 22 gun and his friends with their pellet guns. We drove to an old airfield and the hunting began. If you could call it that. The rabbits would freeze in the beam of the headlights of the car, making themselves easy targets. It certainly was not pleasant to watch and I was beginning to regret my decision to tag along.

The 22 and the pellet guns were noisy, with pellets ricocheting off the old air strip's surface to who knows where. Before long, someone from one of the nearby homes must have called the police and the sound of sirens alerted us to abandon the airfield. Before we knew it, a police chase was on! We sped down a country road, trying to get away from a pursuing police car. When we came to a bend in the road, Richard shouted at me to throw the 22 out the window, which I promptly did. Further down the road, my husband pulled over the car. The police officer pulled in behind us.

The policeman told Richard to open the boot (trunk) of the car. The cop pulled a dead rabbit out and held it up, firmly stating, 'There is no way a pellet gun shot this rabbit!'

After a moment of silence, he angrily continued, 'Where is the weapon that shot this rabbit?'

Richard just stood back, not answering.

The policeman searched the car and nearby hedgerows for a weapon that could have caused such damage to a rabbit. Finding none, he asked Richard for his driving license and ordered us to follow him to the police station where we spent the remainder of that night and all the next morning in a damp, cold cell.

After lunch, we stood in front of a judge and were

promptly fined £700, which we thought was a bit excessive. Richard, of course, tried to explain that we were close to the end of our holidays — and that our money was running out — but that with all good intention, he would forward money to pay the fine upon our return to Canada.

Good luck with that one, Richard, I thought to myself. *Your banter won't work here.*

The judge slammed his gavel down with authority and raised his voice. 'This court stands in jurisdiction until this fine is paid.'

Richard made a few calls and found the money, fast! Later that day, he went back along the country road and retrieved his 22.

The headline of the story carried by the local newspaper the next day read: *Canadian Poachers Fined.*

I started noticing changes in Richard's personality. His style of manners and dress also changed. He had his hair permed, which was fashionable at the time, then he went shopping and bought a leather sports jacket. This new hippy look was topped off by his new habit of smoking dope, especially when we were socializing.

I blamed Morris, our neighbour. Morris had a camper van parked in his backyard and he often would sit inside, smoking weed. He often invited Richard to join him. Morris was an attractive, older man; to look at him you would never guess he was such a dope fiend.

After a hard day at work, Richard would often invite people back to the house for a beer and sometimes a BBQ. Two of our renters, Ray and Mo, often joined us. Ray was a polite gentleman studying ortho-dentistry at the local Uni who got a kick out of Richard's personality. Mo did secretarial work. She didn't drink beer but was a pot head like Richard and Morris, the handsome neighbour. Richard revelled in telling different stories and everyone seemed to have a good laugh.

When Richard suggested I should smoke dope along with him because maybe it would cheer me up, I was surprised that he ever thought I needed cheering up. I never thought I was ever 'down' in any way. But I gave in and tried it. It just made me eat everything in sight and then sleep for a long time. It affected Richard differently. I felt it made him look and sound pathetic, laughing at any stupid comment and being louder than usual.

After staying with us for over a year, my sister and her husband returned to England permanently and, of course, took their little daughter with them. I missed them terribly and then did, indeed, become very down and depressed. My mind often wandered to the fact that I could not have children, and that saddened me even more.

6

MEANINGLESS GIFTS

Even while I sensed some growing distance between Richard and myself, he seemed to want to spoil me with more gifts each passing year.

On my birthday one year, he called me into the backyard. There sat a new Silver Anniversary Corvette Stingray with white leather upholstery – for me!

However, as I was admiring my new four-wheeled passion, another new Stingray was driven into the yard. He had purchased a second Stingray for himself. We had matching cars, except for the fact that his was white with a blue leather interior.

That year, the last year of our marriage, we journeyed once again to England for our winter holidays. This time,

Richard booked a different mode of transport. He had always been a lover of fancy cars and he made arrangements to purchase and take a Trans AM car back to England. The car was beautiful, bright yellow with black leather interior. I believed his intention was to keep the car in England to use whenever we were there holidaying.

We were to drive it to the docks of Old Quebec City where we would meet our ocean liner, the *Stepfan Batory*. It was the last crossing of the year, leaving in November. We had trouble finding our location in Quebec City. Everyone we stopped to ask directions to the docks spoke very little English. Finally, we arrived at the dock. We were the last to board and we almost missed our ship. Once we were settled on board, I found it to be quite nerve racking. The ship's hallways were decorated with photos from previous crossings — many showing the exterior of the ship and its rails covered with thick layers of ice.

This particular ocean liner was first put into service under the Holland America brand. The ship was subsequently bought by the Polish government in June 1968 and rechristened the *TSS Stefan Batory*. There was quite a diversity of languages spoken on the ship, but understandably Polish was spoken most often.

I spent most of the nine days in the cabin suffering with sea sickness. It was horrible — the ship seemed to go sky high atop every wave, and then crash down violently. But on days that I didn't have my head down in the toilet being ill, Richard and I joked around with the other passengers and had a good laugh about our different ethnic mannerisms. Finally, it was time to disembark. Standing safely on land, and taking possession once more of our car, was a great feeling. The Trans AM became the talk of the town when we arrived home. Pulling up at petrol stations always caused a stir.

It was on that visit to England that I truly began to suspect that Richard was being unfaithful to me. I had found a lighter in the car, along with cigarette butts in the ashtray. The butts had lipstick on them, a shade that wasn't my colour. Of course, he denied any 'fooling around,' saying he had just given someone a ride home. But the seed had been sown and began to grow rapidly.

When it came time to return to Canada, I was unsure if I should go home with Richard. Not only due to the signs of his unfaithfulness — but also due to his growing suspicious and unreliable behaviour. For example, one afternoon shortly before we were due to return home, we were staying at my mum's house and there was a knock on the door. Richard answered. There was a police officer on the doorstep, requesting to speak to my husband. Without a moment of hesitation, Richard said he wasn't there, that he had gone back to Canada. The police officer then asked my husband if he (Richard) had left a forwarding address. Of course, Richard said, 'No.'

I suspected the incident had something to do with the yellow Trans AM, but I didn't say anything — neither to the police officer on the doorstep nor to Richard after the officer had left. Our holidays were at an end and we both flew home to Canada. The car was abandoned, or sold — I have no idea. I put it down to another one of Richard's shady deals. 'The least I know the better' was becoming my motto.

Oh, how Richard was changing! A new Corvette Stingray, permed hair, a change of fashion, and smoking pot whenever he was hanging with the boys. On top of these changes, he also seemed to be in desperate need to have the people around him stroke his ego, an ego which was growing bigger and bigger.

At a big house party one night, Richard was sitting on the floor laughing and chatting, a bunch of friends encircling him. I was on the couch talking to another woman but with one ear on Richard and his conversation.

One of the women in the circle asked Richard if he was married and Richard said, 'Yes ... that's my wife sitting over there.'

One of the men had his back to me so perhaps he did not know that I could hear what was being said. He replied to the curious woman, 'You should ask him if he fools around!' And, to my great surprise, she did just that.

'Oh nooooooo ...' Richard promptly replied, much to the amusement of the whole group as they all burst out laughing.

I was so angry I feared I would do something stupid. I stood up and asked for the keys to the car. With a shocked look on his face, Richard handed them to me, and I left.

I drove around for a while and made up my mind that I did not have to put up with his crap. I returned to our house. Upon walking in, I heard whispering coming from the direction of our bedroom. I made my way over and could see Richard's face in the dim light. I kicked the bedroom door open with my foot at the same time that Richard pulled it open. The door smacked him in the nose. He swore out loud and he and his male friend exited the bedroom. I could only surmise that they had been whispering about drugs. At this point, I really didn't care.

I followed him into the living room and confronted him. Without giving an explanation, I announced, 'I am leaving you.'

Richard didn't ask why. He didn't say anything at all. I interpreted this to mean that he didn't give a damn. I went on to say, 'You need to give me $1,000 for my airfare back to England.'

Richard just stared at me, lost for words.

I told him, 'I will pick it up tomorrow.'

I left, slamming the door behind me.

I drove around until daylight, tears streaming down my face as I listened to ABBA loudly in my car, the lyrics of 'Knowing me, knowing you' pounding through the car speakers.

I picked up a coffee at a McDonalds drive through and then went back to the house to pick up my money. The house was empty, but Richard had left the money in the cupboard where we kept our unpaid bills. This set me off crying again as I knew in my heart that Richard leaving the money meant that this is what he wanted also.

After picking up the money, I drove to my dream home where Mo was still one of our renters. Mo and I had grown closer over the time that we had known each other. She was a bit of a pothead and smoked it daily but I felt I had no right to object, considering my own habits of smoking cigarettes and drinking beer.

Within a couple of days, I had returned to England. Alone.

I found a job as a wine waitress at a local restaurant, but it was not long before I missed the exciting life I had had with Richard. After talking to some friends, I realised I may have been too hasty in leaving him and hopping on a plane back to England. I still loved him and wondered how we could possibly put things back together if we were thousands of miles apart.

My brother, who had earlier joined us overseas, had since moved to Vancouver. I was in telephone contact with him often and he knew how unhappy I was back in England. He suggested I return to Canada and stay with him and his new girlfriend.

I was just 25 years old and had only been married for six years. I told my brother that I wanted to fly back to Canada to see if my marriage was truly over. I thanked him and said if things didn't go to plan with Richard, moving in with him and his girlfriend was a good idea. I joked, saying I would probably see him soon.

I returned to Canada and found that Richard had moved residences. He had rented out the first floor of the three-story home that was once our forever home. Mo told me Richard had moved across town and had also hooked up with a girl, someone much younger than me.

Richard's hook-up girl was known as the *Snow Queen* because of her reputation for being a successful seller of cocaine. She had been described as thin with long, beautiful hair. I knew Richard well enough to know he would be very much into the Snow Queen, not so much for her beauty as for access to such a popular drug.

At that point, I felt that even if I tried to get Richard back, I would be fighting a losing battle. I made arrangements to meet up with Richard. I told him I was only there to get some money and then I was going to move away and stay with my brother in Vancouver. Richard had said it would take him a couple of days to get the money for me, so I again stayed with Mo.

Finally, Richard called and said to come pick up the money. On my visit, I could see the signs of partying, which was normal. I asked to use the bathroom, and on the counter I saw evidence of a woman's presence — jewelry and perfume — which made my blood boil.

It was truly depressing for me to see these things — I had been deeply in love with Richard and totally faithful throughout our marriage. I tried to console myself with the fact that he was lousy in bed and that I was now done with his 'Wham, bam! Thank you, ma'am' style.

But the gloves were off. My heart was filled with revenge. Before I went round to pick up the money, I had already decided to take advantage of him sexually. It gave me pleasure to think that he had cheated on the Snow Queen so early in their relationship.

Richard gave me the sum of $5,000, which would enable me to fly out to my brother's place in Vancouver and tie me over until I found a job. The $5,000 was all that Richard ever planned to give me. I figured it was better than nothing.

I went back to the house where I was staying with Mo. I purposely went out of my way to meet up with Ray, the orthodontist renter. I had always found Ray attractive and now I fed the attraction that I had previously denied myself. Ray let me cry on his shoulder and one thing led to another; it was my childish way to spite Richard. Then, I went to find my handsome, weed-smoking neighbour, Morris. It didn't take long for him to pick up on my flirtatious vibes and soon we were having sex in his spare room. I then set my sights on Richard's favourite lawyer, whom I had met many times before.

And I felt justified in all of it. In my mind it was simple – infidelity was the only method of payback that I knew would bother Richard. Not that anyone would tell him — I was never going to tell him about it, and I was certain that neither Morris or Ray would. If we were in the USA, no doubt his favourite lawyer would have 'taken the 5th.' No, this was all about inner satisfaction.

After drinking heavily and following Richard from a distance, I finally saw him with his tiny, skinny, long-haired girl through what I presumed was the window of her home. I sat in the car, staring. She seemed to be performing some sort of dance or form of exercise. It was really weird to watch and I put it down to her being messed up on weed.

I sat back in my car. Once again, tears rolled down my face. In my drunken stupor, I decided I would be okay. I was young, I could get a job. My brother would help me get resettled. I would be fine. As I drove away that night, I felt different … stronger and more determined.

My aunt encouraged me to talk to a lawyer — which I did. After telling him about the houses Richard owned (plus the trucks and fancy cars), he said it looked good for me to receive half of his assets. That was until the lawyer did his homework and told me that Richard had large mortgages on all the properties. He felt that Richard must be using the rental income to pay for his lavish lifestyle, rather than paying down the mortgages.

After clearing my next move with my brother, I pulled myself together and booked a flight. I couldn't wait to step onto that plane. My brother was waiting at the airport with open arms. I was on the west side of the country and I thought I would never look back.

7

I WILL MAKE YOUR
TOES CURL

I settled in with my brother for an eventful six months, miles away from Richard. I applied for a job as a nurse's aide and when they called me to say I had the job, I was over the moon. It was in a private hospital for wealthy people undergoing plastic surgery.

One of the patients had just gone through a full-face lift and I was fascinated with the process. She looked like an Egyptian mummy, lying there with only slit openings for her eyes and mouth.

'Why would you do that to yourself?' I asked her.

She told me it was because a friend of hers had had the same procedure and it made her look ten years younger.

I could tell she was trying to smile under all the bandages

as she said, 'I promise you that I will come back when all the bandages have been removed and show you the before and after.'

She did exactly that when the time came and brought pictures of herself before the surgery. 'Wow!' was all I could say. She did, indeed, look ten years younger than her pre-surgery self. I promised myself that when I got older, I would do the same thing. I was just under 26 at the time.

My brother was living with Lucy, a woman who was friendly and welcoming, bubbly and uplifting to be around. I felt she was perfect for him, as I had always thought of him as slightly introverted like Mum. They were great in every way, including encouraging me to go on dates with friends of theirs.

One Friday after work, the women I worked with were getting together for drinks, so I went along with them. The four of us started our evening in the lounge of a very elegant — not to mention expensive — hotel. It was not long before a group of well-dressed men attached themselves to us. Drinks and snacks kept coming to the table. Obviously, money was no problem for them.

One of them was particularly interesting. His name was Harry and he told me that most of the men in his group played basketball for the Harlem Globe Trotters. He, though, was a musician with the Vancouver symphony orchestra. He said he played a variety of different instruments, but mostly saxophone. I was impressed, to say the least, and immediately besotted.

Harry had a charming personality and made me laugh. He was suited up handsomely and smelled of expensive cologne. Even his teeth were beautiful.

At one point, he leaned in close and whispered to me, 'I

bet no one you have ever met in your life can make your toes curl like I can!'

It was obviously a double entendre and, of course, I was taken in and intrigued. This man Harry, who was claiming that his sexuality was up there with the best of them, was amusing me to no end with his forward banter.

After an evening of laughter and drinks, we decided it was time to head home. Harry took me to the lobby and gave me a lingering kiss goodnight. We exchanged information and arranged to meet the following night. My friend and I had discussed sharing a cab as we lived in the same direction. Harry opened the back door to the taxi and gestured to us to get in. He then handed money to the driver, 'Take the ladies to wherever they need to go.'

The next evening, he took me out to a beautiful restaurant and then we were off to a nightclub. We went in through the back entrance to avoid the line-up at the front. That manoeuver did not go unnoticed by me. I guess I was easily impressed, just as I was impressed with Harry's heavy tipping. Because of that tipping habit, people were anxious to please him wherever we went. He seemed to be very well-known in his circle. He made me feel like I was the only woman that mattered, simply because he was so attentive.

He introduced me to cocaine that same evening. I was willing to try it, mainly to see what all the fuss was about the drug. Strangely, I felt safe in the hands of Harry and he seemed to know what he was doing. He showed me how to squeeze tobacco from a cigarette, add cocaine to the middle of it, and then pack the tobacco back in.

Damn, that drug made me feel good! It seemed to be quite harmless and it released a personality from somewhere inside me that I did not know existed. I was suddenly more open to dancing, which I had never been before. I felt all of my inhibitions leave my body. I felt like I wasn't real.

At the end of that evening, we went back to his apartment, which was spotless in more ways than one. Completely devoid of furniture except for a mattress on the floor that was decked out with luxurious bedding. Candles and bubble bath surrounded a large, clean whirlpool tub in the bathroom. Everything looked new, including the fluffy white towels.

We were not inside the apartment long before Harry began explaining that he had recently broken up with his long-term girlfriend and that he had left her with everything. He said he had just bought the essentials for the place we were in, and that he was still in the process of making a fresh start. It all seemed credible to me.

A couple of weeks passed, and I felt things were going great. We were learning more and more about each other and spending all our available time together. Harry was always at his apartment when I finished work and we fell into the habit of drinking wine and using special cigs. Harry also taught me how to snort cocaine. He was excellent at giving massage and my toes always curled.

We swapped life stories. I was truthful about my past. I told him all about my husband Richard and how things had gone so terribly wrong. Harry was very comforting and empathetic, saying that Richard's loss was his gain.

Harry's story seemed believable. He explained that the

evening he met me he had just returned from Europe having been away for two months on a tour with his fellow musicians. He went on to say that he was now taking a well-deserved break. He spoke deeply about his love for music and his job.

Harry asked me to move in with him. I was so taken with his lifestyle that I immediately said yes … but only on condition that he meet my brother and his girlfriend for their approval. Dinner arrangements were made.

My brother approved, and all was good. I was excited to do my own thing and get out from under him and his girlfriend. They had been good to me, but it was time to leave them alone.

I moved in with Harry and left my job at the plastic surgery hospital. Harry had convinced me that there was no need for me to work because he would look after me. I was convinced of that because he would take me shopping in some of the fanciest stores; places where they had seats outside the changing rooms, which was quite uncommon back in the day. 'Try this on … and this,' he would tell me as he picked things out for me. And when I did try them on, he would say, 'That looks so beautiful on you … We'll take it.' My life revolved around fine clothing, fine dining, heavy drinking, lots of special cigarettes, cocaine, and sex.

Then, one morning when I was sleeping late, the phone rang and woke me up. It was Harry.

'Go and pick up the dry cleaning,' he said. 'I'll be home soon, and I need my black suit.'

'Nooo!' I said in a groggy voice, 'I'm sleeping.' Then, I put the phone down.

Within ten minutes, he was in the apartment, pulling me

out of bed. In an instant, he held me naked up against the wall with his hands around my neck.

'Don't you ever, ever, put the phone down on me again,' he shouted close against my face.

I was in total shock, shaking and crying, failing to understand who this horrible person was.

Yet as fast as the attack had started, it ended, and Harry was apologizing profusely. He ran me a bath, made me a hot drink, lit a cigarette for me, and said repeatedly how much he loved me and how truly sorry he was. He said he was stressed and had money problems because of his ex-girlfriend and that he had not been paid by the symphony for a long time.

We got high and had sex for the rest of the day and night. But he had seriously frightened me, and I started thinking about how to get out of the relationship. In my more sober moments, I began to question the truthfulness of Harry's story. But after a few drinks and a couple of special cigarettes, I wanted to avoid any heavy discussions. I especially never wanted to see the ugly side of him again.

After having Harry scare me so badly that morning, sleep never came easily. My mind ran away with itself, and I had a deep-seated dread that Harry wasn't who he said he was. The cigarettes were no longer innocent liberators of my inhibitions. I was convinced the coke was to blame for most of what I felt was wrong in my life.

But how was I to stop it? Harry had stopped asking me if I wanted a special cigarette, especially when we were home. He would automatically line up the coke and expect me to indulge. I did say, 'No' once or twice, but he would never take 'No' for an answer. He would line up the lines and nudge me, saying 'Come on, your turn.' I felt that if I refused, it would make him angry and I was scared of that side of him.

On the same week the attack happened, I had made plans to have lunch with Lucy, my brother's girlfriend, and a couple of her friends. I kept asking myself, 'Should I say something to them?' I decided that discussing my problems was not a good idea. It would embarrass Lucy in front of her friends … I would tell her when we could be alone together.

When they asked me about Harry, I stupidly found myself putting him on a pedestal, even bragging about him. I did not mention that Harry didn't possess furniture nor that I had never seen even one musical instrument. I certainly did not mention cocaine. I felt lost, with a disturbing feeling that I was somehow sinking.

They acknowledged my beautiful dress and how good I looked. So, instead of talking to them about my concerns regarding Harry, my insomnia, my paranoia, I stupidly just told them, 'Thank you, Harry bought the dress for me.' The conversation moved away from me and ended as a fabulous lunch filled with laughter and good food.

At the time, I didn't know there was a term for what Harry was doing to me. He was grooming me for prostitution. He was not what he had professed to be. He was not my boyfriend, and he was not a nice man.

8

TAXI

I never stood on street corners. I was a high-class prostitute. Connections with customers always happened in lounges of downtown, high-end hotels. I don't say that with any kind of pride. I know that prostitution is exactly that, no matter where you sit or stand.

Calling it 'high class' just made me feel better about the situation I had gotten myself into. In a strange way, it was my pride that made me go along with everything. I did not want to let my brother know I had covered certain things up, that I had failed, or that I had been completely wrong about Harry.

With the benefit of hindsight, I now realise I was desperate to be wanted, loved, and protected. I truly wanted what I felt everyone else had — a happy relationship.

Besides — while I was with Harry, I really felt that I had nowhere else to go. He had quickly morphed into being my pimp, no longer an impressive man or a loving boyfriend. I felt trapped.

A shiver of fear ran through me as I watched his face contort into the face I feared. He went on, counting off different expenses. Our drugs. Our food. Our rent. Things he had paid for both of us. I had contributed nothing. 'Nothing!' he shouted. The only way for us to keep up our lifestyle and not get evicted was for me to get out there and help. If I did it his way, sleeping with men, the money would come easy and fast.

I cannot remember actually agreeing to it. Cocaine and booze had taken over, making me ever so malleable and easily manipulated.

Anyone who has fallen into the sleazy world that I fell into, without a doubt, would remember their first 'trick' with great clarity — it is a sobering experience because you don't know what to expect.

After following his instructions to a tee, I left the john in his hotel room and called Harry so he would know that things had gone smoothly. His instructions to me had been to agree to whatever the client wanted, get the money up front, and not to permit kissing — ever.

Going into the hotel lounge for the pickup, I was not nervous or scared, or even apprehensive. For reasons I cannot explain, I was excited. I did not see any danger in what I was doing, partly, because I was high. Even after having been raped at 14, I had never thought of men, in the general sense, as my enemy. But that feeling would soon change.

Initially, I was quite pleased with the way the whole scenario went down. The few drinks I had consumed ahead of time probably had something to do with that. I found the man that approached me and asked if he could join me for a drink quite attractive and personable. After ordering us both drinks from the waitress and charging them to his room, I started to relax a little. It took him no time at all to ask if I was a 'working girl.' My response was just a grin. He nodded and said, 'Okay then, let's go.' We finished our drinks and proceeded up to his hotel room.

I never mentioned to this man that he was my very first customer. I wanted him to believe that I knew what I was doing.

After we had finished, as instructed, I left the hotel room to call Harry and let him know that I had the money and that I was okay.

However, as I reached the lobby and looked in my bag, to my horror, the money was gone! I was sure I had put it in my bag. Panic stricken, I had no idea what to do. For several moments, I leaned against the wall near the elevators, fearing how Harry would respond. His ugly side had reared its head a few times and I never wanted to give him a reason to be upset.

I decided to go back to the room and ask if I had dropped the money on the floor. The client was still there and let me in, then he proceeded to give me a lecture – a huge lesson from my first 'john.'

'When you use the bathroom, always take your bag with you,' he said. Then, he laughed a little, smiled a little, and gave my money back to me, plus an extra fifty bucks. He wished me good luck and we parted.

He had gone into my bag while I was busy in the bathroom and helped himself to the money that he had paid me.

Drinking went on day and night in that world. It made me think often about what Elizabeth Taylor purportedly said about her excessive alcohol consumption: 'I could always drink more than most women.' I drank like Elizabeth. Life was just easier if you were high or drunk.

Sitting alone in a lounge was my pickup place for johns. I chose them by accepting a drink before anything 'professional' transpired. If they were not dressed nicely and did not have shiny shoes and a nice smile, they were likely to strike out, even before they sat down for a drink.

I always turned my money over to my pimp, who, in turn, called me his No. 1 earner. All the while, he continued to pamper me and tell me how much he loved me.

Of course, I thought. *I bring in big bucks for you.*

What I learned from the many different men I encountered was that most were rather stupid and let their 'little' head rule their big head ... and their wallets. It was an eye opener for me to realise that my body was an excellent source of currency. Feeling wanted by so many men had an enormous effect on me. In the saddest of ways, it made me feel loved.

I had read stories of women and girls being beaten and/ or doing tricks for drugs and money, yet there I was — caught up in a world that was equally frightening as it was disreputable. Not knowing how to change things, I just went along. Money was given to me by the johns, which in turn I passed to Harry — which always made him a nicer person to be around.

All the johns weren't as considerate as my first one. Or as normal. One man wanted me to burn him with cigarettes. I refused and promptly walked away. Another one wanted me to stand on a glass coffee table wearing nothing except my stiletto heels. He also suggested, 'If you sit naked on the glass coffee table, I will lie down underneath it and have a front row seat!' Men with sick fantasies that had watched too much porn.

I quickly learned the lingo — words and phrases that I had never heard before ... such as *golden showers ... cock rings ... anus dildos ...* the growing list made me realise what a sick world I had found myself in.

One night, I did something stupid, something I had been warned never to do. I let a john convince me to go back with him to his home instead of staying within the safety of a hotel room. We reached his home and proceeded to walk through the front door. Upon realising the electricity was out, he referred to his wife as the *bitch from hell*. It was not totally dark, so I could see through the dim light that it was, in fact, a nice big home with fine furnishings. He told me that he and his wife were in the process of a divorce and that she had moved out into their daughter's home until the lawyers had sorted things out. He went on to explain that she had cut the power off out of spite.

We drank heavily, and then after the job, I said I wanted to order a taxi and leave. He went downstairs, supposedly to get my money, while I continued to get dressed. Then I heard him shouting, 'You bitch, you stole my money!'

I ran to where he was to convince him otherwise

and tried to help him find the missing cash — wherever he had previously hidden it. All we had was a flashlight, so it was difficult, to say the least.

I was scared. He was slowly losing it, demanding to look in my bag and to search me. He had convinced himself that I was a thief.

He slapped me, called me names, and dragged me to the floor by my hair. I had to think fast and try to calm him down before the situation worsened. I struggled through my tears to get him to think, to go over in his mind just where he would have put the money.

Then, he removed a cushion from a sofa and pulled out a plastic bag full of one hundred dollar bills.

What a relief!

He turned to me and saw that I was crying and that my leg had been cut during the scuffle. He apologized and tried to hold me and convince me to go back upstairs with him. He said he would double the money if I did.

By that time, I knew I was dealing with a nutbar and thought fast on my feet. I said I had to get home to relieve the babysitter that was with my two-year-old. I told him he could come to my apartment where we could continue the job if he wished. Of course, it was all lies — but the present situation had sobered me up fast and I was thinking more clearly. I managed to convince him to agree to my suggestion.

A taxi came and I gave the driver an address that was nowhere near where I wanted to go. The john sat in the front seat with the driver. Once on our way, I instructed the driver to please stop at the gas station coming up on my side of the car.

'I need to pick up cigarettes,' I said.

As soon as we stopped, I ran inside and shouted, 'I need help! Call the police! I have been attacked and he is outside!'

At that point, I caught a glimpse of myself in a display mirror. I had a swollen face, my dress was torn, and I had holes in my stockings. Silently, I vowed then and there that I had to leave, to get away from this sick, sick environment before either a john or my pimp killed me.

It did not take long for the police to show up with sirens blaring. The taxi took off with the john, and thankfully, I never laid eyes on him again.

By then, I had composed myself somewhat and decided that Harry would go absolutely crazy if I turned up with a police escort, so I refused to give the police officers any name, address, description of the man, or other information about what had happened or where I had been.

I told them I was sorry to have bothered them and that I needed a taxi to get home. I figured they probably knew it was a trick gone wrong. I refused a ride home from them and, finally, they reluctantly called me a cab.

I was afraid they would follow me so I stopped off at a pub, where I went into the bathroom to tidy myself the best I could. I went into the bar and had a couple of drinks before going outside to hail another taxi to take me home.

When I finally met up with my pimp Harry, he scolded me for stepping out of the safety of the hotel and then proceeded to pour me a drink, pull me a bubble bath, and gave me a massage and a cigarette. Oh yes, I craved those special cigarettes more and more.

That night, I realised that I was deep into the game – too deep. All the fancy dining and the privileged back-door entries to the finest night spots were not making me feel special anymore. I wanted out. I needed out! Thoughts of how to escape began to consume me.

9

ALMOST ROAD KILL

One night, my pimp Harry announced that we were going to a house party. He told me that many other pimps and their No. 1 girls would be there.

Upon arriving at a very large, nicely decked-out apartment, we were served cocktails and I was left to mingle with the other girls. Harry went around, greeting people he had not seen for a long time. I found out later that some of the pimps weren't local and had come in from other provinces.

In talking to a few of the girls, I realised they had been in the business longer than I had — and soon the stories began to flow about Harry.

'Has he beat you up yet?'

'He has a reputation for beating his women.'

'One of his girls fell off a balcony, full of booze.'

'You should come and work for my pimp. He is lovely and would treat you like a queen.'

Four different comments from four different girls. I wondered if the stories were true or said just to make me leave my pimp and to go and work for theirs?

Worrisome thoughts swirled in my mind. The sooner I changed my life the better.

As I made my way to the bathroom a bit later, a man in front of me dropped his wallet. I picked it up and caught his attention. I never considered doing anything else. It was a reflex action.

'Excuse me,' I said. 'You dropped your wallet.'

Unknown to me, my pimp was not far behind and joined us. The one who had dropped his wallet praised me highly.

'What a great girl you have here,' he said to my pimp, '… so honest!'

Later, when the party was over and we were leaving, the man was still telling my pimp how lucky he was to have me.

As I stood there waiting to leave, the two men talked about me like I wasn't there. I felt completely invisible. Like I was just a thing … an object that these pimps carried around with them. We could be worn out, literally thrown away, changed for a better, nicer one — or just left behind. I felt these feelings might be an effect of the drugs I was using, but they were real thoughts in my head.

When we arrived back at the apartment, I threw off my shoes and went to the bathroom, realising that I had just started my period. When I came out, my pimp was angry, 'You were stupid to give that wallet back to the guy who had dropped it. You could have just picked it up and kept it, no one would have been any wiser. There was no one else around to see.' He further berated me with each new sentence. 'You should go out to work right now to make up for your stupidity!'

I told him I could not do that because of my period. He proceeded to rant about how other girls went out to work regardless, using sponges 'up there.'

When I began to cry, he went into the kitchen. I heard him snort a line of coke, then he came back into the bedroom in a lighter mood. He told me to stop crying, saying, 'It's okay, put your shoes on. We're going to Seattle to see my supplier. I'm almost out of coke.'

I just wanted to go to bed and sleep. I certainly did not want to go to Seattle. In fact, I did not want any of it anymore. I was living with a real Jekyll and Hyde, loving one minute, violent the next. But I had no voice and no choice. I had to go.

I was quiet in the taxi as we set out for Seattle, hours away by car. Thoughts of the stories I had heard at the party were going through my head, especially the one about the girl going over the balcony. After the episode over the wallet, it was easy to believe there could be truth to such stories. What I knew for sure was that this pimp of mine, a man I had been so impressed with when we met just a month earlier, was absolutely nuts!

Like me, the taxi driver was quiet. The pimp had pushed money into his hand and told him where to go. I was sure the driver sensed that this customer was high on something.

We had been driving for about 30 minutes when the pimp realised I was silently crying. While shoving me hard up against the door, he began raising his voice, telling me to 'Stop your crying! You want to go back?'

Then, to my horror, he reached over and opened the door. While holding onto my hair, he then pushed me so far out that only my head was keeping the door open. I squeezed my eyes shut in fear. When I opened them just seconds later, I saw nothing but the road speeding by under me. The road's surface was mere inches away.

'Stop the car! Stop! Stop!' I screamed.

Seeing what was going on in his back seat, the driver quickly slowed down and, in a surprisingly calm and quiet voice, he said to the pimp, 'Come on man, think about what you are doing.'

My pimp told him to mind his own business and to keep driving. I went completely silent with fear as he pulled me back into the car by my hair. I pulled the door closed. Harry told the driver to turn around and take us back to the apartment.

The return was quiet. No one spoke. I kept to my corner of the taxi, taking quiet breaths in and out so as not to cry. Back in the apartment, he left me alone only after reinforcing our respective roles in the world, forcing me to give him a blow job. It could not have been any clearer about who and what I was. I cried silently into my pillow, visions of the road flashing past my eyes as my mind searched for ways to leave this horrible, horrible man. I couldn't bring myself to go to my brother. I was too afraid of what he would say to me or what he might want to do to Harry. My brother was an ex-rugby player and a strong man. I didn't want him to get into trouble with the law for taking up my revenge.

I eventually slept and was woken by Harry, a cup of coffee in hand, pretending that everything was fine. I pretended too. I certainly did not want to change the mood or give him an excuse to hurt me again.

10

GOOD COP BAD COP

At that time, I had been regularly meeting with one particular john. He told me he had his own company, building houses. In turn, I had told him my standard line — I was putting myself through university — which seemed to please him. More than once he said, 'I would hate to think all this money I give you is ending up in the pocket of some bad-ass pimp.' He would often ask me to stay overnight and offered more money. I always said, 'No' and would think of an excuse. I certainly never mentioned his request to Harry.

I found him kind of creepy — he always wanted to hug me too tightly, abnormally tight. But then, it seemed no one in that world was normal, whatever 'normal' was. He constantly upped the ante to encourage me to stay overnight. It crossed my mind that maybe he was so besotted with me I could use him as my ticket to freedom. I told Harry that my regular john wanted overnights with me and that he would pay the going rate. Harry agreed and set the fee — money was the key to everything to my pimp. My plan was set in motion.

My john was extremely pleased that I was accepting his proposal to do an overnight stay with him. Arrangements were made and as soon as we had settled into the hotel room, I broke down and told him the truth ... that he had been right. I did have a pimp and there was no university. I said I was scared for my life, that the pimp I was involved with was crazy. To my utter surprise, he told me he had been lying as well. He was not a builder. In fact, he was an undercover police officer!

He said he had witnessed many deaths in the prostitution racket, thanks to bad-ass pimps like mine. He explained how such men take their girls with them from province to province so that they have no friends or family nearby to turn to.

Undercover police officer! I was truly amazed. Over time, he had gotten sexually 'caught up' with some of the girls, but especially with me. He said he would help me get away in return for my silence about his dishonorable conduct as a police officer. With that, he had tears in his eyes, which made me believe him completely. My escape would take place on a night I knew my pimp would be busy elsewhere. My john would take me back to the apartment where I would collect some of my clothes and my passport. He would then take me to the airport and I would fly home to England.

As planned, the john and I pulled up outside the apartment. The car came to a full stop and I gasped in horror when he pulled out a gun. My heart pounded hard and fast. Like a clap of thunder, that gun brought home the seriousness of what we were doing, and the real danger I was in. I was frozen in fear until my john made me snap out of it, saying, 'This is just a safety measure. Go! Get your passport if nothing else.' I thought, *What if he has to use it? What if my pimp also had a gun tucked away somewhere.*

In the apartment, I quickly threw things into a suitcase, grabbed my passport, and raced back to the safety of the car. As I shut the door, a wave of relief flooded over me. At that moment, I hoped more than anything that I would now be safe.

He kept telling me it would all be okay. 'He can't hurt you now,' he said. 'He won't even find you. It will be alright.'

After a brief silence as we both caught our breath, he asked, 'Is there anything you need to do before I take you to the airport?'

I said I needed to call my brother to let him know that I was leaving. To this day, I cannot remember what I told my brother during that call, other than the fact that I was leaving and returning home to England.

As I look back on those moments and the weeks previous, it seems like it happened to someone else. Sometimes, I sit back and wonder if that woman was really me. I often think, 'Did that really happen? Did I do that?'

I took a deep breath on the way to the airport and closed my eyes for a while, believing I had turned the page on that nightmare of a life.

However, in the few hours we had been executing my escape, the john had begun to think of the excursion to the airport as a 'date.' He suggested we stop by the banks of the river and take in the view. Then, he suggested we stay overnight at a motel en route and book my flight from there. Even though he was saving my life, I felt sick to my stomach. But going along with his fantasy was the price I had to pay for my freedom.

He wanted to hold my hand and kiss me like some long-lost lover. There had never been a single kiss between us before, but that night was obviously different in his eyes. He gave me a photo of himself and said he hoped that one day our paths would cross again. Not surprisingly, I started to wonder if this 'hero' of the day also had a screw loose. Maybe I was not being saved but just getting into more trouble with a different man. It seemed to be my pattern.

I felt I had no choice but to go along with the love-sick puppy. We got up the next morning and I was happily surprised when he took me directly to the airport. He went to the counter and purchased my ticket — which was the only reason why I had been so subservient. He also bought me a book to read, and handed me some extra cash. We said our goodbyes and I thanked him for helping me and told him that I would never forget him, although, from my perspective, my memory of him would be for all the wrong reasons. He had tears running down his cheeks. I obviously meant something more to him that the average call girl but he represented nothing to me but the horribleness of my life. I could not wait to get to the lounge area for a couple of hard drinks. I hated myself for thinking the way I did, knowing this man had probably saved my life. Yet, at a deeper level, I hated him. I could not wait to get on that plane and be done with all the many aspects of selling myself.

Shortly after takeoff, I opened the book the policeman john had given me. It was *Deep Throat*, by Linda Lovelace. I had never heard of the book before that day. As I flipped open the book to the first page, my disgust for the man who had been my saviour grew. The book was about giving head and how successful this woman was because of her famous blow jobs. Tucked in between the pages was his photograph that I had purposely left behind in the hotel room.

He had such a good, respectable profession, and yet he seemed possessed by sex. To this day, I do not understand his reasoning for giving me a photo of himself. On one hand, I was certainly grateful to have met him and found myself feeling empathy for him. On the other hand, I detested him and what he falsely represented. I tried to push the negative feelings aside, hoping to convince myself that I would be forever in his debt, regardless of the fact that he was obsessed with the seedy world of prostitution.

I was not yet 28 years of age and I had been happily married, then divorced, then hooked up with another man who I thought was the answer to my dreams. That dream man abused me and sold me to other men. I had only been his girlfriend for a handful of weeks before the month of hell began, a month that gave me a lifetime of unwanted knowledge.

Finally, I was free of all of it, relieved and hopeful of a new start.

11

DO I HAVE TO COME
TO YORKSHIRE?

I was staying at my mum's, which was always the case when I travelled to and from England. My mum never asked many questions, but when she asked me about my past love interest or why I had left Vancouver, I had no choice but to answer with lies. I hated myself for that, but I couldn't do anything else.

It did not take me long to find a lawyer in York to move forward on my divorce from my soon-to-be ex-husband. The lawyer told me it would cost me more than it would cost Richard as I was the one initiating the divorce. Luckily, enough time had past so there was no contest required from Richard. I signed documents to change my name back to my maiden name and an affidavit confirming that I didn't want any monies from Richard, now or at a later date. My divorce was absolute August 30th, 1985. I secretly cried on and off most of that day.

The third day after I arrived, the phone rang. Harry's familiar voice on the other end of the line said, 'Hello, my Yorkshire pudding. Do I have to come to Yorkshire to bring you back?'

Frozen, I hung up without saying a word. Motionless, my mind raced, wondering what to do. He obviously had found my mum's phone number on the phone bill, but would he really come all the way to the UK to drag me back? I decided I need to shake his call off, shake my past life with him off, and move on.

I quickly moved on to a familiar face to hang out with, to go drinking with every night. Phil was a friend of Richard's. I was surprised we were so compatible, even though the connection between us was far from anything profound. We were both in character – he liked buying drinks and I liked drinking them. But we did have fun together, and what a change that was from the life I had just left as a 'working girl.'

Phil was renowned for being a tough guy and I felt safe around him. I decided to tell him what had happened to me since I saw him last. During that evening of confession, we drank and drank. He told me that I wasn't to worry. No one would touch me. Period.

One night when we were partying at the home of one of his friends, Phil asked me to marry him! Being thoroughly drunk at the time, my brain was not truly working and I said, 'Yes!'

The next morning when we stumbled downstairs after a night of sex, he proudly announced to his friend and host that we were going to get married. His friend was jubilant and shook

Phil's hand, then leaned over and gave me a kiss on the cheek. The friend was over the moon with the news.

Later that day, I visited a girlfriend and told her I knew that I did not want to get married again. What was I thinking? My only excuse? I was drunk when I accepted his proposal.

Her immediate, somber reaction was to say, 'You have to call him over here and tell him … sooner rather than later!'

Though I hated the thought of it, I agreed it was the right thing to do. He came round to her house and we went into the kitchen for privacy. With genuine tears in my eyes, I told Phil, 'I am so sorry. I can't marry you. It was never my intention to hurt you. We both had a lot to drink, and we had so much fun, I think we both got carried away in the moment. But I don't even know what country I want to live in let alone whether I want to get married again.'

His eyes opened wide as he grabbed me by my throat. My feet were slightly off the floor. With his other hand he poked me in the chest and said through his teeth, 'You are supposed to have a heart in there … but you don't possess one … anywhere!' Then he let go of this grip on me and walked out.

He didn't hurt me, I knew it was a just a reaction on his part. Maybe he had told other people about us getting married and now he would be embarrassed. I felt terrible and disgusted with myself, knowing I had hurt such a good friend so badly.

12

BOOZE,
BIKERS, BAHAMAS

Impetuously, I decided to go back across the Atlantic and promptly did so. I moved back in with Mo, who was still a tenant in my dream home. Mo had turned out to be such a good friend, always there to give me a warm bed and a place to be whilst I got myself sorted out. She was a kind woman and very sensible in the way she thought about life – which was just what I needed at that moment.

I managed to secure a job in a nearby restaurant and was feeling pretty good about my choices which included life without unstable, love-sick men.

Shortly after my return, my cousin Christine and her boyfriend asked me out for drinks. We were sitting at a table in a nightclub when a bunch of people my cousin knew joined us. One of them promptly asked me to dance.

'No thank you,' I said, 'I don't dance.'

With that, he moved his chair away from the table, held his hand out to me, and said with a sexy smirk on his face, 'No? No! You say no to me? Never! Nobody says no to me!'

This man was charming and exceptionally handsome, of Italian descent. *'Mmmmm, I like this,'* went through my head.

We began an open relationship. I think the terminology that best described it, at least back then, was 'fuck buddies.' We hung out together at least once a month and when we were in quiet mode — nursing hangovers — we watched movies together. I told him he reminded me of Sylvester Stallone, which was quite fitting because at that time the whole Rocky series was popular. My Rocky was a true player, taking advantage of his handsome looks with the young chicks in the night clubs. We got along well, especially in the bedroom. I was never demanding of his time and vice versa. We just clicked and came together over and over again.

I never told him about my two months of craziness as a hooker in what I refer to as 'a different world.' In fact, it was not until years later that I realised I had been a victim throughout that entire episode of my life. Only after that realisation, could I talk about it at all. It was just like when I had been a victim of rape with the bus driver so many, many years earlier. Eventually, I learned to forgive myself.

I started hanging out with an old friend, Libby. We got along so well we agreed to move into a plush, two-bedroom high-rise apartment together. I went to see it and it was beautiful, fitted with white shag carpeting, two balconies and two bathrooms, plus indoor and outdoor swimming pools, shared sauna facilities, restaurants, and an adjoining night club. It was like staying permanently at a holiday complex.

I had just taken a different job as a bartender in the beautiful lounge of a new hotel and things were looking good financially. The lounge seated 150 people and the tips were excellent. I thanked Mo, my pot-smoking roommate, for helping me out and then I moved into the luxury apartment with Libby. At the time, Libby was a dental assistant with very different hours of work than I had. She worked days and I worked evenings, but whenever it worked out, we hung out together.

Another girlfriend, Michelle, was a coworker at my new job. She had two children by her first husband. They had long been divorced. Now she was in and out of a physically abusive relationship. She and her partner fought all the time, and the fights were usually started by her, not him. One night, we were partying at her house. It was late and we were all drunk. She and her lover got into a huge argument and she picked up the stereo and threw it through her own living room window. To say they both had tempers would be an understatement.

In spite of her hot temperament towards her partner, Michelle and I got along well. She introduced me to many 'firsts,' such as the introduction to The Los Bravos biker gang. Arranged through a friend of a friend of hers, the bikers were stashing garbage bags full of who knows what in her basement.

Michelle had many responsibilities - two children, a dog, a cat, and a mortgage. Her ex-husband was a nice guy who would often take the children for the weekend, giving Michelle and I lots of time to party.

After a night of bar hopping, Michelle and I ended up at a late-night diner. When two tall, handsome, leather-clad bikers walked in, I asked Michelle if she had ever slept with a real 'biker.' She said she had not. It didn't take too much flirting from us before we were invited to join them at their table and from there to a house party. We drank, we had sex, and we left. In my mind, it was mission accomplished! We slept with two handsome bikers.

By that time, my drinking had gotten way out of hand. Even though I rarely became sick or suffered hangovers, I knew that drinking a 26 oz. bottle of rum on a daily basis was bad, really bad. Michelle had no problem keeping up with me or, quite possibly, I had no problem keeping up with her.

The lounge where Michelle and I worked was situated within the hotel and had its own entrance. It was a popular place; the local professional football team was based in the stadium close by and when professional wrestlers were in town they would book into the hotel.

Michelle, having worked there for some time, had been entrusted with a set of keys with which to open and close the place. Eventually, she figured out that her bosses did not have a clue what was going on with the lounge stock. Hotel management only counted and kept track of the actual booze, never the cocktail ingredients.

With keys to the lounge, it was very easy to bring in our own bottles of booze and blend it in with the lounge stock. Michelle decided how many bottles and of which kind we were to take in. This enabled us to sell our own cocktails and keep the money. We made money left and right. It was great. Michelle was the mastermind behind the scheme — I was the perpetual follower, naively going along.

In those days, if I had a moral compass at all, it must have been broken. We started with a couple of bottles of vodka and rum as those were the most popular alcohols to mix into cocktails such as Caesars, Pina Coladas, or a Planters Punch. There were twenty-six shots in a bottle of alcohol. That meant that we sold twenty-six cocktails from our own stash of booze. With our tips, wages, and this illicit revenue, we were making good money.

I was intrigued with the whole biker scene and learned that prospective members of the gang were called 'strikers.' They had to earn their 'colours,' which were emblazoned on the back of their leather jackets. This was accomplished by carrying out the instruction from their superiors until they were deemed ready to become fully fledged members, earning the right to wear the club jacket.

My ears perked up one day when Michelle told me the Los Bravos leader wanted to hold a meeting at her house. Although I was still living at my cosy apartment downtown with Libby, many a weekend I would stay at Michelle's, especially if she was having one of her parties. I made a point of being at Michelle's the day this meeting was to take place. I was curious as to what the boss of the Bravos looked like.

The leader walked in and sat down. He explained how two of his strikers had gotten themselves into serious legal trouble and needed to stay low. He asked Michelle if they could stay at her place for a while. They would be no trouble, he told her, adding that they would be respectful toward her, and anyone else who was part of her household.

The gang leader spoke with such authority. His mere presence and demeanor demanded respect. Even though he looked to be quite chunky under his leather garb, he was not a very big man, which led me to believe that he must have earned his leadership role through his ability to talk and to organize.

It was not long before the two strikers walked in. Michelle and I froze, afraid to even glance at each other. They were the same two bikers from the diner that we had met and gone to the house party with a few evenings before. Both of us were silent, not even giving a friendly, 'Hi, how are you?' We certainly didn't breathe a word of our dalliance with the handsome bikers. We didn't even acknowledge that we had met. They acted like we were strangers as well.

The two bikers were given their instructions and told they could stay on the top floor of the three-story house. They stood there with their heads down, respectfully listening to orders from the gang leader. He told them to be undemanding and, most of all, thankful that they had been given a home to use as a hideout.

It did not take long for me to become the gang leader's bed partner. He had made no bones about finding me attractive. I was also still seeing my Italian stallion, so things were getting pretty hectic in that department. I did not want them to meet each other.

I decided there was never a better time to take my roommate Libby up on her invitation to go on a holiday. I felt I needed a break from the madness that I had once again found myself in.

Libby and I went off to the Bahamas and had a ball. While we were away, she confided in me that she was being romanced by a new guy. When we returned, I met him at the nightclub next to where we lived. Speaking from experience, I told her he had all the traits of a pimp. She became angry, insisting that I was wrong and that he was a wonderful person.

I was glad that we worked opposite hours as our conversation had caused us to distance ourselves from each other. Not only did I believe that her new guy was a pimp, I believed he was possibly an associate of my ex-pimp.

Unfortunately for Libby, I was right about my assessment of her new boyfriend. She eventually figured out what his intentions were and told him she never wanted to see him again. He stopped his pursuit of her. I am glad that our friendship was able to weather that awful time.

I could not help but think that it was my association with the Los Bravos gang that made the pimp do a U-turn out of Libby's life. It is well known on the streets that pimps and bikers do not mix well, but they hold a certain respect for each other's territory.

Michelle and I eventually lost our jobs in the hotel lounge. One day, the hotel managers called us both into the office and told us that considering its seating capacity, the lounge should be making more money than it was. They told us that they knew that there was thievery occurring, but they couldn't prove it.

We both moved on to a steakhouse restaurant and bar further down the road. However, that job did not last long either because we drank more than we served. We were confronted shortly after a shift when we had been drunk on the job. Our excuse was that it was Christmas Eve. Again, we were fired. I slept most of the next day. When Libby came home after her shift at the dental office where she worked, I kept the fact that I had been fired from my job due to my heavy drinking.

Losing my job twice in a row hit me hard. What was I going to do? I decided I would just drink, and I did, also realizing there was no longer any doubt about it ... I was a functioning alcoholic, just like my dad.

13

CHECKING OUT

I scoured the papers for something I could do that I could call a real job. My eyes kept returning to an advertisement. The ad read: *MASSAGE ATTENDANTS WANTED - Full training will be given, no experience necessary.* The job sounded interesting and, more importantly, like something I could do.

Eventually, I decided to phone and find out what it was all about. The man at the other end of the phone had what I called the 'gift of the gab,' and reminded me of Richard, my ex-husband. In an overly friendly tone, he told me I would be under no obligation to take the job, but to just come down and take a look. He went on to say that all the staff wore uniforms and that they were provided for a small cost. The pay was per hour for the time we were booked, plus the full amount of any tips given to us by clients.

He gave me the address, along with directions, and I agreed to come and meet him at his office. I set off to find the place, but wandered further into the back streets than I planned. It was a part of town that had a reputation for being rough, a part of town where I had never been. Feeling lost and disheartened, I had no choice but to return to the apartment before the sun set and I was even more at risk. Once home, and feeling pretty down, I decided to get drunk and maybe try again the next day.

As I was about to settle in with a bottle of rum when the intercom buzzer went off.

Libby answered the intercom. To my utter and complete surprise, it was Richard. Libby pressed the button for the buzzer and asked him what he wanted.

'Ask Sandra to come downstairs. I need to talk to her. I am not leaving until we talk.'

Listening to the conversation over the intercom, I told Libby, 'No, I don't want to talk to him.'

She had met Richard many times before and willingly went down in the elevator to find out what his problem was. It wasn't long before she returned, saying, 'It seems to me like he wants you back. He said he's not leaving the building until he talks to you.'

I nearly choked. It had been a long time since Richard and I had split up and I knew I could never go back. I simply was not the same person he had married, nor the one he had tossed aside six years earlier for the Snow Queen.

I reluctantly took the elevator down to see him. He said

we had to talk outside in the open and not go to his vehicle as it might be bugged by the police. Apparently, he had got himself involved with drugs and all the associated nonsense.

'*What a shame,*' I thought, '*both of us have been caught up in the fast lane and it was eating us up.*' I knew the man I had fallen in love with, and travelled thousands of miles away from home with, would want nothing to do with me if he knew even half of what I had become. I got the feeling that he just wanted a familiar face to talk to. I sensed that he was perhaps a little nervous, or even paranoid, as to what was going on in his life – scared of deportation or being picked up by the police. He finally left and I went back to the apartment. I sat in my bedroom, feeling sorry for us both, crying, and drinking rum.

In the silence of the early morning hours, I took every pill I could find in the bathroom, then I returned to my bed convinced that what I had just done was the best thing for me … to just check out from the whole mess that was my life.

Libby found me before it was too late. What an angel! She had no reason to check on me, but she had. Maybe she heard me sobbing.

When I woke up, I was in the hospital and my stomach had been pumped. I felt stupid and, at the same time, sorry for myself. How could I have let myself get so low, so insecure?

I had had all those men in my life who wanted to be with me, but I knew that all they really wanted was to use me for their own sexual gratification. At that point, as far as I was concerned, that was true of all men.

'Well, fuck them all!' I said out loud and, believe it or not, right or wrong, I drew strength from that thought.

When I was released from hospital, I swore my inner anger to secrecy, and pushed the whole mess to the farthest corner of my mind.

With a new mindset, it was time for me to find a job, again. I made a concerted effort to stay away from the bar scene, though I never stopped drinking. I just slowed down. But I was more aware than ever before that I had to take control, somehow.

14

A NEW CHANCE

That ad for a massage attendant kept jumping out at me from the newspaper, so I called. Again. The same man answered the phone, still so friendly, full of life. I told him that I had walked past the 7-11 store as he had instructed but from that point on his instructions had been confusing. He gave me the directions again and repeated, 'Just come down and I will show you around.'

On the second attempt, with clearer instructions, I found the right place. It was in a very seedy part of town. I sheepishly opened the door from the street and looked inside. I opened another door directly in front of me and found myself looking up a steep set of stairs. I nervously climbed my way up to the top, unsure of what I would find. There was a large, smoked-glass door. To the left of the door was an intercom. I pressed the button and shortly after I heard the door lock release. I walked in. The welcoming atmosphere beyond the smoke-glass door was quite different from the stairway. At the end of a meticulously clean and stylishly decorated hallway, I could see a man getting up from behind a desk to greet me.

A couple of pretty young women, passed me in the hallway. They politely said, 'Hello', as they walked past, leaving the scent of expensive perfume trailing behind. The sounds of laughter and chit chat came from a room with a sign on the door that read 'Staff Only.'

The man held out his hand for me to shake and then directed me to his office. I took a deep breath. I could feel myself starting to relax.

'Take a seat,' the man said. 'Sorry you had so much trouble finding us.'

He said his name was Bob, then asked me if I would like a cup of coffee.

'Yes, please,' I replied.

He buzzed the intercom on his desk and ordered two coffees, which were promptly brought to us by another, very attractive girl.

'Hello,' she said, then turned and left. I looked across the desk at Bob and thought to myself that he was quite handsome. He certainly had a beautiful and friendly smile.

But I still had my guard up and I guess he could see that I was pretty tense. He asked if I would like a cigarette. I took one from the open package he offered. He stood up and leaned across the desk to give me a light.

I had never known anyone before, or since, who could make a person feel so comfortable in such a short time. We made some small talk and then he stood up.

'Let me show you around.'

Each room had its own theme and was fitted with a whirlpool tub, a massage table and a shower. Mirrors interspersed with framed pictures of women in different stages of undress adorned the walls.

Then, we were back in the office with more coffee and cigarettes. I cautiously filled out a very simple application form and found myself spilling out my life story to this stranger, who said all the right things in all the right places to put me at ease.

He told me the basic rules of the business. The most important one was that there was no 'Full Service' with clients, as in sexual intercourse.

'*Good!*' I thought.

He told me that he had taken a massage therapy course and received his diploma. He went on to say that the business itself was fully licensed with the city and that all his staff were eighteen years or older and they were each individually licensed with the city. Full massage training was given to all attendants. Uniforms were provided, for a fee, and were to be worn over one-piece swimwear. My uniform was to stay on at all times, unless I was in a room fitted with a tub, in which case I could wear a swimsuit. The hourly pay was paid out by cheque once a month. Any tips given in cash were my responsibility for declaring at tax time. Aside from the uniforms and swimwear, I would also be responsible for paying for my licence. Bob said he would even drive me to the licensing office and help with the forms. The most important rule, which he stressed above all others, was that any drugs or alcohol found on the premises would result in the owner of the items being fired immediately.

Bob said I would need a set of photographs for the albums that were kept at the front desk. The albums were used by the customers to choose an attendant for their session. One of the albums was on his desk and I asked if I could take a look. At his nod, I flipped through the photos and then gave a sigh of relief. None of the women in the photos were nude. Some of photos were just face shots and all of the women in the photos were wearing one-piece swimsuits.

Bob gave me an approximate figure of my anticipated monthly income, which would vary depending on how good I was at massage and, more importantly, how good I was at letting the customer think that I was not just in the room for his money. Bob said, 'It is important for the customer to feel you are genuinely enjoying his company. You need to treat a hundred-dollar tipper the same way you treat a five-dollar tipper.' He smiled. 'That is a true art form in itself! It's like good acting.'

He went on to say that he was the one who did the training for all the staff. He looked at his watch and said that if I had time, and if I had decided to come onboard, he could begin my training right then. This way, I could come in for my first shift the following day. I stood up and told him that I did not want to commit to anything at that moment, but I would sleep on it and call him.

It all sounded too good to be true — the money, the hours. But it was just two years since my horrific experience with Harry, the pimp, and I knew deep down that some sort of sex had to be involved — somewhere, somehow. As I made my way home, I thought about everything that Bob had said.

Libby had earlier remarked that she didn't want to renew the lease — she wanted to move closer to her place of work. She asked me if I would move with her, and I told her that I didn't want to live that far away from the city centre. Not only was I running out of money, it appeared that I would soon be homeless.

There was something about Bob that made me think in a positive way about the whole opportunity. He had a way of reaching out with his caring words of advice. In the interview, his words had come across in such a heartfelt way that it had brought me to the verge of tears. He pulled my innermost thoughts out into the open and had me talking about my past with such ease. I had only read about what good could come from talking to a therapist, but I imagined it would be very similar to my experience that took place that day.

The phone rang just as I returned to the apartment. To my surprise, it was Bob. He told me to forget the job offer for a while, and then added, 'Just let me take you out for dinner.'

He picked me up that same evening wearing a checked blue, awful, awful suit … and I told him, as politely as I could, how horrible it really was. Later, I also told him in a jovial manner that I was also not impressed that his business associate had come along on this 'dinner date.'

Bob introduced me to is ex-business partner, David. He was a much older gentleman, very polite. They had been friends for many years. Over dinner, I learned that David's wife was adamant that her husband get out of this line of massage therapy as fast as he got into it. Bob had fully expected to have clients come to him for a legitimate massage treatment, but the majority of those possible clients that walked through the door asked for girls to deliver the massage. That was when David's wife insisted that her husband get the money back that he had invested with Bob.

Bob must have been very determined to be successful. He paid David back and stuck with the small building space that they had rented together. While building his own massage business, Bob also had part-time jobs as a store detective, a beer vendor, and even a clerk in a 7-11 store. He said he always had a vision of success. I was told that at one time, Bob had three different jobs at the same time. One job he took just to learn the ropes of the massage world — an overnight cleaning job in a massage parlour down the street from his location. Some of the staff there would work past midnight and he picked their brains about how the business was run. It didn't take long before Bob learned everything he needed to know. Slowly, his business became known for its luxurious sessions and beautiful girls.

He found himself very busy and went out of his way to keep rules in place so as to not break the law. Over the years, regulations and laws came and went as the city's lawmakers went back and forth with what the laws should and shouldn't be. Bob's biggest rule was that all staff members had to be over eighteen. If he was caught with underage staff, he could get closed down. His second most important rule was there was to be no using drugs or alcohol while on site. All staff had individual city licenses, as heavy fines were in place for working without one. These were checked on a regular basis by the city's licensing department.

Massage parlours were usually hidden away in the

dumpier parts of the city and were well known for selling more than massage. These parlours were often nicknamed 'Rub and tug' – rub for the massage, tug for the extra sexual favours. Bob said he wanted to change that way of thinking, he wanted to change the way the business was described, but also to give customers an experience to remember simply by pampering them and surrounding them with beauty. He wanted the main focus of the sessions to be about the massage. Exceptionally clean surroundings was the key to having repeat clientele. Large whirlpool tubs, dim lighting, soft music, hot oil. Plush linens and beautiful women who had a high interest in giving an excellent massage and zero interest in 'Full Service.' Bob said some massage parlours offered escort services where a customer would call for a girl to be sent out on a date to his hotel. This was never of interest to Bob. *Escort* meant, and still does, to go out on a date to provide sexual service. *Full service* meant sexual intercourse. Bob wanted to only have in studio sessions which meant none of his staff went out to meet clients. If a staff member was caught or known to see customers outside the business, and therefore eliminating desk fees, she would lose her job.

The evening out with Bob and David was full of good food, good wine, and laughter. It turned out Bob was quite the entertainer, telling stories of his life experiences.

Then, it was time to leave.

'Are you not going to invite me in,' he asked, as we reached the front entrance of my apartment building.

'No,' I said. 'I will see you tomorrow for training.' We both smiled at each other and he left.

Thoughts spun through my head that night. I had a sense

that I was being backed into a corner — not by Bob personally, but by life itself. Bob was impressive and I certainly found him handsome. He was different. He came from the Caribbean and was full of jokes and laughter. Thinking about the character that I had spent the evening with put a smile on my face.

After a somewhat sleepless night, I convinced myself I would check out the massage opportunity. Bob seemed like a kind and thoughtful man and if the work and situation was different from what I was expecting, I would just leave. What did I have to lose?

15

RULES, RULES, AND
MORE RULES

I was introduced to what seemed like a plethora of rules on my first day in the new job: keep one foot on the floor at all times while giving a massage; no lying down with customers; no kissing customers; no letting customers kiss or massage you; no soliciting, which meant no asking or negotiating for money; don't forget to show interest in the customer's life, but don't be too personal; and never ask where a customer lived or if he had a wife.

'The way to succeed,' Bob emphasized 'is to let the customer know that you are not in the room for his money.' Bob then introduced me to one of his female staff members and asked her to show me where the lockers were and where I could hang my coat. I was grateful to be able to ask questions from someone who was working directly with customers.

So far her answers lined up with what Bob had told me.

'What is your stage name?' she asked.

'My stage name?'

'The name you use here. The one the front desk will use for booking appointments. Using a name other than your own creates a distance between you and the customer. You don't want them knowing too much about you. '

'Oh, I hadn't thought of that," I said.

From her, I learned that the more tantalizing a story I could tell while giving a massage — such as being a nymphomaniac, or loving sex with other women, or loving to talk unadulterated filth — the easier it would be to do the job at hand. The key to keeping customers coming back was giving a 'heavy' massage. This simply meant using more pressure, which was more difficult — not to mention more tiring — than a light touch massage. She went on to say, 'Some girls think it doesn't matter about the massage and they get lazy in session. Then, they wonder why they are not as busy as others that have learned the art of giving a good massage.'

If a customer chose you out of the album as their attendant, you were to take him to the treatment room and start filling the tub, making sure that the temperature was correct. Then, you would ask if he would like a coffee or a soft drink. After taking his order, inform him, 'Go ahead and take a shower and I will return by the time the tub is full.'

Once you return, set his drink down on the table and set the timer for the whirlpool jets. Ten minutes for half hour session and twenty-five minutes for one-hour sessions. Go ahead and join him in the tub while wearing a swimsuit. Start your massage, beginning with the feet and working your way up the body to their shoulders. After the timer expires, ask if he had enough of the water. After towelling him dry, invite him to lie on his stomach which will enable you to give him a back massage.

'The ambience is created by dimming the lights, staying silent and tuning in to the music and focusing on giving a good massage. After the initial heavy massage, use your fingertips like feathers, creating a goosebump effect, primarily around his backside and inner thighs. Do not shy away from his bottom — men love people massaging their bottom. Then, in the sexiest voice possible, ask the client, "Would you like to turn over?" The client will comply, of course, and if he doesn't have an erection — well then, you have simply done a lousy job with your teasing feather touch massage.

She went on to tell me. 'Then we play games, asking the client a question like, "So, is there anything else I can do for you today?" If the client wanted more than the bath and massage they had already paid for at the desk, they might typically reply, "What can I have?" Respond back with a question such as, "What would you like?" Answering a question with a question is yet another art form in the business. Remember,' she said sternly, 'asking and negotiating for money is solicitation, which is against the law. If the customer is looking for 'extras,' they will ask. Your response should be, "What did you have in mind?"'

'Usually they will reply with something like, "I want to go down on you, I want to eat pussy... or maybe get laid ..." then your response is "No, no, no. Think of something else." She continued her advice. 'Many customers get upset, even angry, when they realise that we are not a full-service establishment.'

Sessions were timed to exact minutes. If you were early or late, there were consequences in place. You were fined by the desk (which was a direct payment to Bob) if you missed a shift. If you were scheduled for a weekend and didn't come in to work, you were fined double. These fines were no joke — $100 for missing a shift along with a full week off work. You were told to, 'Go ahead and party for the week.'

Clients who had been there before would know what services were available. These 'regulars' also knew to put their tips out on to the table.

She explained, 'You would be stupid to trust any customer to tip for service at the end of the session. If you didn't get tipped, you were a fool – and he was an arsehole. Having the customer's tip in your possession gives you the control. This way if a customer gets out of hand, you can give him a warning, like "Listen, if you do not behave yourself, I will leave the room and you will have to talk to the person in charge at the desk." A customer, upon realizing his behaviour was not just between himself and the attendant, would usually settle down.'

At times, customers were demanding and rude, especially if they didn't get their way. Bad behaviour would be when a man would insist on trying to kiss you or trying to put his hands into your swimsuit. If she had had enough of telling him to stop and the customer wasn't listening, the attendant would just walk out . The customer would be left with an erection as she left the room, bringing the session to an abrupt end.

If a man was known to create these type of problems with staff on his regular visits, he could be barred altogether. These customers often got away with too much bullshit when assigned to an inexperienced attendant who hadn't followed the advice to always get her tips upfront. She would find herself possibly giving in to a customer's demands so as not to lose out on receiving a tip. This was all her fault for simply not getting the tip before the beginning of the session.

The rule was 'No Full Service' so an attendant would lose her job if she was caught doing more than she should.

Most of the staff chose to work at this establishment because they didn't want to do Full Service. A girl might even report on another attendant if she saw the other attendant come out the room with a large tip in her hand, as this might indicate full service.

Bob would randomly question the girls as to how their session went, how big a tip they received, and whether the customer left happy.

There were things that Bob did that I thought were very wrong but I was in no position to call him on it. For example, he had regular customers that he would use for setups. He would give the customers large amounts of money that was marked with a pen. If the girl came out of the session with the market money, she was told that she had been set up and that she had failed the test. The money was taken away and she was then brought to tears, pleading for one more chance to keep her job. The customer got free sex, the money was returned to Bob, the attendant got nothing. This was all so that Bob could know who he could trust.

However, it was only during my own training that I realized that these rules only applied to customers and the other attendants, and not to Bob and myself.

One of the rooms close to the front desk was called the

Bubble Room. The large tub had no jets and could be filled with bubble bath. My training took place in this room.

Bob did not have a shy bone in his body. As soon as we entered the room, he stripped naked and entered the tub. I was asked to sit on the edge with my feet in the water.

He made the point that I would be more comfortable if I changed into one of the staff swimsuits. I replied, 'I will keep my own clothes on, thanks.'

With my bare feet dangling in the water, he proceeded to show and tell me how to give a good foot massage. Then, he instructed me to slide around to the back of him to massage his shoulders while I sat on the edge of the tub.

He talked about possible breakdowns in timing. For example, when a customer had paid for an hour, I was to try to keep him in the tub for half of that time. When he exited the tub, if he picked up a towel, I was to say, 'Here, let me do that for you.' Then, I was to instruct him to lie on his stomach while I proceeded to give him a massage. This had all been told to me by the staff member – the woman that had spent an hour answering my questions — but I let Bob ramble on to see if there were inconsistencies with her instructions or any other little details I needed to be aware of.

Now, I became the customer. Bob asked me to remove my top and lie on my stomach so that I could learn his back massage techniques. I agreed. The massage was informative and very relaxing. Before I knew it, he had turned me over and peeled the rest of my clothes off. He knew exactly what he was doing and I was so turned on that I was more than willing. The hot oil, the ambience of the music and the dimly lit room, combined with the expertise of his teasing hands and expertly given oral sex, truly blew my mind.

Then, he pulled my legs towards him to the end of the massage table and over his shoulders. He entered me hard. After a few seconds, he moved away from me to the tub and rinsed himself of. I lay there wondering what the hell had just happened. I had never had anyone, not a boyfriend, husband, or otherwise, ejaculate that quickly.

As he got dressed, he looked at me with a smile and said, 'Remember, never do that with customers … we do not do full service here.' He dressed quickly, and said, 'I'll see you at the desk.' He left the room, leaving me in my post-coital daze.

In the interview, Bob had convinced me that my life would change for the better. And it did! Before long, I was literally throwing money in the air. I could not believe there were so many men out there who just wanted the company of a woman, to be touched by a woman, and then to give her money for that experience.

I found that men have many reasons for wanting such a service. Not all men are strikingly handsome, nor God's gift to women, nor even capable of successful dating. Some businessmen told me they did not have time to wine and dine while also trying to climb the corporate ladder.

As I had been told on that first training day, the sessions were well timed and controlled. I also learned for myself that, sexually, men will always want what they think they cannot have. The better the attendant was at teasing, talking dirty, massaging, caring, and joking, the less choice the man had but to climax fast and sometimes involuntarily.

Of course, every customer was different. Commonsense, not to mention street sense, went a long way. The other girls often told stories about different customers, especially the ones that were known to give them a hard time.

You have not lived until you have shared a staff room with ten other women, sharing information about male genitals and stories of different experiences – all normal topics in this business.

It did not take Michelle long to jump on board. The interest rate on her mortgage payments had shot up to 17 per cent and she was really struggling to keep up. She and I had discussed my moving into her house when the lease at the apartment with Libby expired. Michelle thought that if she could work more shifts, it wouldn't take much time for her to get caught up with her bills. If we worked opposite shifts, I wouldn't have to pay rent and she wouldn't have to pay a sitter. It was a win/win situation!

Once I moved out, Libby and I kept in touch and continue to do so to this day. I will never forget her for how she saved my life. I still think of her as my saving grace, and that I wouldn't be here if it wasn't for her checking in on me - and for this I am forever grateful.

16

BOB THE STALKER

When Richard decided to return to England permanently, he left a trail of unpaid bills and loans. The bank was unwilling to give me a loan for a car due to the fact that I had no credit rating. Bob was more than willing to co-sign my car loan. I was very grateful to him and thanked him profusely.

I am not sure if Richard was deported or if he went back home to England of his own free will — all I knew was that he had left a trail of people looking for him. I found it ironic that when we had first left England, I was the one that had begged to go home and now, years later, it was he who was back in England, and I was not.

He had taken his junkie girlfriend with him. This move gave her an opportunity to become a new character and to leave her 'Snow Queen' reputation behind her. In the meantime, because of Richard, I had people tracking me down that were trying to track him down. I had legally changed my name back to my maiden name in England, but now needed to do so as well in Canada — as Richard's bad decisions continued to hound me.

What a mess we had made of our once-promising lives. It made me cry just to think about it.

On the other hand, things could not have been better at the massage parlour. It didn't take long for me to learn all the tricks of the trade. I got a kick out of the fact that men, in general, always wanted what they could not have. Being the one in control, gave me quite a high. However, I was always true to the rules, mostly because I believed that it would be foolish to lose my job by giving in to a big tipper, no matter how attractive that tip, or the client himself, might be.

Our local competition was less than a mile from our building and offered full, naked, sex — along with other options many people had never imagined possible. It was known throughout the city that their approach was 'anything goes.' Word of mouth travelled from customers that had visited both places. We knew that our place was busier, was well known for being cleaner, and had many more girls to choose from. The competition did not have the ambience of the tastefully decorated treatment rooms. We were, overall, just first class.

In hindsight, as sad as it seems, I relied on that comparison to remind me that I had it pretty good working where I was — I did not have to have intercourse with any of those men.

In the early weeks of my working, the other girls started

giving me a hard time because I was busier than they were. It was said around the staff room that I must be giving 'Full Service' or that I was busier because the boss was suggesting that customers choose me. It was true that I did have a collegial relationship with Bob and that might have influenced his assigning of clients.

I joked and played around with Bob in a way that was similar to how I did with my customers and, before I knew it, we were meeting up for breakfast on a daily basis. This was easy and convenient as the breakfast restaurant was very close to where we worked.

It wasn't long before Bob picked up on the fact that I was interested in working the desk. He began treating me as his right-hand person, teaching me how to do payroll. Eventually, I picked up every aspect of running the place. As a result, the distance between the other staff members and I became more apparent. I didn't care. Learning the business was more important than what the other attendants thought of me.

Bob and I had conversations during our daily breakfasts about our respective families. Because he was never home, I found it hard to believe that he had a wife and, at that time, a newborn child. Once when I asked about his wife's tolerance regarding him rarely being at home, he said, 'There is just one captain of a ship … and my wife knows that this business gives us the lifestyle we have so she never bothers me when I tell her that it is work that I'm out there doing.'

At that time, Bob was still training all the staff himself. The first time he asked me if I would like to learn to train others properly, to learn massage techniques, I jokingly responded, 'With or without the orgasm?' He laughed too, but didn't answer the question. Our first training session was very professional and I did pick up some new massage techniques, but it didn't take long for it to turn into another full-blown sexual experience, except this time he wanted to kiss me — and I let him.

From that day forward, when someone new started and needed training, Bob and I would do the training together. Bob stripped off into the tub and I was responsible for showing massage techniques, beginning with the feet. We would go through the training session, giving the new staff member all the knowledge that she would need to start work.

I began to realize Bob was falling in love with me. Although I liked him, I wasn't in love with him. I just wanted to keep my job because it provided me with a wonderful lifestyle. I was learning the business and Bob continued to give me more and more responsibilities. It wasn't long before I was given a set of keys and told to open if I was on a day shift and told to lock up if I was on an evening shift. This enabled Bob to come and go as he pleased.

Michelle and I went out drinking and partying any time we could — especially when we had days off together. She had met some owners from another massage place in town and heard that their lease was up and they wanted out of the massage studio. Michelle made arrangements to meet up with the tenants at their location. It was in an even seedier part of town than where we were presently working, but we both felt we could still make the business work in that location. We left the conversation uncommitted, saying we needed time to think about it.

However, it was not long before Bob found out about our meeting. He tried to persuade us to abandon the idea. He said bikers were after the same place and that it was dangerous to cross them. He pointed out all the negatives … the costs of the license, the linens, the water bill, and on and on. He was purposely trying to deter us from getting involved in our own business … and it worked. Subsequently, Michelle and my thoughts of getting into our own business were never realised.

Bob became fully aware and concerned that I might disappear from his life and he said as much. He now knew about my desire to own my own business and began to pay more attention to me. He would often show up at the same place where Michelle and I would go out nightclubbing. Finally, I had had it. I threw the office keys at him and yelled at him, 'You have no business following me around. Stay off my stomping grounds during my personal time!'

My courage to confront him was an alcohol-induced one-off. The next day, all was back to normal, breakfast as usual. He just laughed at me and handed me back the keys.

After that, however, Bob would often say, 'I will make you love me.'

17

LIAR

It was wonderful to have my own money. My next trip home to England, I had a gold credit card in my pocket. I took my dad shopping. It made me so happy to be able to give to him. I loved to spoil him with new clothes. He had started with his A.A. meetings and his outlook on life and relationship had changed. He was almost humble.

Mum, however, was a different story. It was hard for her to accept my buying her even a cup of tea when we were out together. Because she never asked for or wanted anything, I could only give her things gradually, over a number of visits. I did this by making the home where she lived into one filled with beautiful furnishings.

I was still not completely free of my ex-husband. He felt it necessary to phone me and tell me how disappointed he was that I had slept with his close friend and then accepted an offer of marriage from him — even though I had declined that offer the following day. I found that behaviour strange. When we were together, I had never even looked at another man. My response to him was quick and concise, 'Hey, I never professed to be an angel!'

I had become damaged goods, to say the least. I think he was shocked at my sharp reply and must have wondered if he was talking to the same woman he had married. He was not! I had changed almost beyond recognition.

He had taken the Snow Queen back to England and made a home with her. He also had a growing family that I was very envious of. Sometimes I would think how nice it would be to live back in England. I missed my family and friends, but how could I possibly go back — only to be faced with no job, no home of my own, and the ever-present conversations revolving around my ex-husband's success? Since returning, he had made several wise investments and everyone was talking about what he was buying and selling and how young and pretty his new wife was. Even my own family was entranced with all the gossip about how Richard was doing so exceptionally well.

My favourite auntie would invite him and his wife into her home for tea. She would ask him what he was buying or selling at the time, and Richard loved to talk about his ever-growing property. When I would go around to visit her, she would repeat everything he told her. I couldn't tell her that hearing about Richard was upsetting, she was in her late seventies and seemed to enjoy the inside scoop of the gossip.

Yet, as strange as it may seem, I felt some inner

satisfaction when Lorraine, my long-time friend, and her husband arranged with Richard to make up a foursome for dinner. I was nervous, not knowing what kind of questions were going to come my way. The conversation centered on Richard and his accomplishments, which made it easy for me to swerve away from personal things regarding my life. The evening must have been costly for Richard, as he insisted on paying for the beautiful meal.

It was almost a perfect evening. It gave me great satisfaction to know that the shoe was on the other foot. Richard was cheating on her and this put a smile on my face. The evening taught me that I still loved Richard, but – there was no going back .

With the help of Alcoholics Anonymous, my dad was finally getting sober. Sadly for him and the rest of us, his sobriety came too late. It was my older brothers that stopped the mayhem that Dad created on a daily basis. They stood together at the garden gate and told him that he had to leave and get help. My mum couldn't take any more of the abuse that went along with living with an alcoholic. I had only lived away from England a couple of years when all this was taking place. I was sorry that I couldn't be there to help when my mum suffered her mental breakdown due to Dad's drinking.

Dad started writing and telling me his many regrets, mainly his wish to have stopped drinking years earlier. He wished my mother would forgive him, especially now that he was getting sober. My dad would talk about how lonely he was and remind me to write him as often as I could. Later on, we took to posting cassette tapes back and forth. His letters and recordings were full of news about family and the weather. I talked to him about Bob and his successful business, which I was directly involved in. I left out the part about my actual work, but I told him that Bob was married but was a good friend who helped me out with many things. I told him — and the rest of my family if they asked — that I managed the place. If any more details were asked, I said that I worked in a relaxation centre, just like a spa, then quickly changed the subject.

When I returned from that last trip across the pond, as we used to say, I discovered that Michelle had rekindled the relationship with her ex-boyfriend. Michelle told me that she was selling the house and moving to a different province. After she moved, I tried many times to get in touch to keep the lines of communication open, but I never got a response. I was certain her reconciliation with her ex included her never having contact with me again.

With Michelle, my partner-in-crime, now out of my life, Bob and I became closer. He helped me with a lot of things, such as purchasing furniture and renting a downtown apartment. When I was married, such things had always been arranged by Richard, so I took to Bob's helping hand easily, and gratefully.

I had my own place, and a job that paid well. However, in spite of my efforts to move forward, Bob was always quick to tell me that if it wasn't for him I would be in a gutter, or dead from alcohol abuse. He was good with his choice of words, making me feel indebted to him, telling me that he was the only reason I could turn my life around.

18

HEAD OVER HEEL
IN LOVE

One day at work, I felt a very strong attraction to a new customer... and the feeling was mutual. His name was Dennis. He came in more and more regularly and would leave if I was not available. Against all of Bob's rules, I started meeting with him on my days off. On weekends, we went away to his cabin at the lake. He told me he was in the midst of a separation and would be getting a divorce. I had fallen in love for the second time in my life. I knew Dennis felt the same way, We started to make plans. I could now see an opportunity to live a normal life.

Initially I was under the impression that Bob was happy for me. He overlooked my relationship with Dennis, just warning me to 'Keep it quiet.' No doubt Bob thought this relationship would blow over. When I declined to participate sexually with

Bob and to no longer do training sessions with him, he knew that this was more than just a fling.

I was so caught up in my love affair with Dennis, I was unknowingly making Bob very jealous. Things started to change dramatically after I told Bob that Dennis and I were in love and that we planned to move to Red Deer, Alberta, the city where he was brought up and where his parents still lived. I had taken a trip out there with Dennis and found it to be beautiful. I didn't meet his parents on that trip, as they were elderly and Dennis said that I would meet them all in good time. Soon after sharing that bit of personal information with Bob, I got a call from Dennis. He told me someone had called his wife and told her that he was seeing a woman from a massage parlour. His tone of voice told me he was not happy. In fact, he sounded very angry and upset.

I tried to state the obvious as nicely as possible. If he was getting a divorce anyway, and his wife was now aware of what was going on, then everything could move forward more quickly. He said, 'I don't want my marriage to end like this! I certainly don't want my kids, even though they are grown, to hear about us before the divorce is final.'

Just as quickly as it had started, it was over between us. I went to Bob for a shoulder to cry on. I poured my heart out, including that I had begun to hate working the sessions with men, and that I had truly thought Dennis was going to change my life. He assured me that, indeed, everything could change, that I could work full-time as a manager. That certainly cheered me up, No more sessions! I would finally be getting a proper pay cheque for managing the business.

I thought about what had happened with Dennis. Who

could have called his wife? It never entered my mind that it was Bob as he was always so willing to help me in so many ways and had seemed to be accepting of my relationship with Dennis.

But eventually, I had to ask Bob, 'You didn't have anything to do with that, did you?'

'Who do you think I am? I wouldn't do such a horrible thing to you! Maybe it was one of the girls.

That sounded reasonable. I had learned that in this business, women can often be jealous, even mean.

That night, I went home, still upset about the breakup. I discovered things were missing from my apartment, things that Dennis had bought for me. As soon as I could, I told Bob. He called my lover and told him to put the stuff back within 24 hours or he would lose more than his wife. He then told me what my 'lover boy' had said in reply, and claimed it was a direct quote: 'Come on, you know she's just a piece of ass.'

To this day, I do not believe that Dennis said those words. I knew him well enough that he would not talk like that. He was well educated and spoke very intelligently. He had an excellent job and was respected in his field of finance. That first day that we had met was his first experience with a massage studio of any kind. I became certain that Bob was responsible.

Bob and I had taken many trips away. On one occasion, he invited me to go to Denver, Colorado to look at a state-of-the-art invention called a Floating Tank, which was a self-deprivation tank. After trying it, he quickly fell in love with the concept and ordered three units. I admit, those 'floating' tanks, as they were called, were really cool. You stripped down and climbed into a coffin-like contraption full of warm salty water, where you would float, often falling asleep to music. In as little as twenty minutes, you could feel refreshed and relaxed, as if you had had several full hours of sleep.

A couple of weeks after I had lost what I thought was my second love, I was keeping myself busy, learning my new full-time position. I was now working twelve-hour shifts promoting the float tanks. At the desk one day, Bob handed me a small parcel that had been delivered by the postman. Excited, I opened it, thinking it must be from England. Instead, it was a letter from Dennis along with a cassette tape with recordings of our favourite songs.

I started to tear up as I read the letter. It was an apology, telling me that he was sorry and that he would like to see me as soon as possible to better explain himself. Bob was hanging over the desk, reading the letter over my shoulder. I could sense that Dennis' letter made him angry. I definitely wanted to meet up with Dennis, but I put up a front with Bob, implying that that was not going to happen. He announced he was going for a floating session.

When Bob had been in the tank for an unusually long time, I feared something was wrong. I walked in and lifted the coffin lid, waking him. He climbed out to the edge of the tank and put his face into his hands.

Standing over him, surprisingly concerned, I asked if he was okay. He looked up at me and cried like a baby, then told me he loved me and that he did not want to lose me. He said he wanted me to be devoted to him exclusively. He said he was sorry he could never leave his wife, but he would look after me. At that moment, I was gullible enough to believe he truly loved me, so the pact was made and I did not respond to the letter from my knight-in-shining-armour.

When Dennis received no response to his letter and tape, he decided to just show up at my door. My heart fluttered as I looked through the peep hole to see his six-foot, two-inch frame holding a bunch of roses. I nervously opened the door and let him in. He grabbed me and kissed me passionately. I did not resist. He held me tightly for what seemed like a very long time. Then, looking at me intently, he asked if he could take me to dinner so that we could talk.

Suddenly, there was another knock at the door. I looked through the peep hole again.

'It's Bob!' I said as my heart quickened.

Dennis bolted for the bathroom and locked the door.

I opened the front door and stepped into the hallway. I bluntly told Bob that Dennis had just shown up to talk and was about to leave. Bob's eyes opened wide as he pushed me aside to get through into my apartment. He took a quick look around and then began pounding on the bathroom door. Dennis never said a word while Bob unloaded a torrent of obscenities.

'When you leave here today,' he yelled, 'make sure this is your last visit to this building.'

I convinced Bob to leave, promising that I was not going to entertain any of Dennis' wishes. I told him I would meet with him shortly at the office. He left, but he was still very angry.

The thought of reviving my relationship with Dennis crossed my mind, but seeing Bob's flare up — which I interpreted was all in my defence — reminded me of all the good things that

Bob had done for me. I remembered Bob's tears and the promises that we had both made.

However, Dennis's arrival at my door, roses in hand, convinced me that Bob had been lying when he said Dennis had called me a '*piece of arse.*' It was also what convinced me that it was Bob who had called Dennis' wife.

However, at the time, it was comforting to believe that Bob truly loved me. Soon after that incident, he took me on holiday to his home country in the Caribbean and introduced me to all of his friends and family members. We had a marvelous time, and I didn't hear from my knight-in-shining-armour again for many years.

One day, when my son was twelve, I bumped into Dennis at a carwash and introduced him to my son, telling my son that this man was a good friend that I had not seen for many years. Dennis had kept his handsome physique and good looks and my heart fluttered again. I learned from chatting with him in that brief five-minute encounter that he had divorced his wife and had married his secretary.

He sheepishly asked me if we could meet for coffee. I thanked him and apologized, saying I was still with Bob, and it would just not be worth the stress of rocking the boat.

He asked me if my son was Bob's son.

'Yes,' I said.

We went our separate ways for the last time. I often wonder, though, when sitting alone with my thoughts, '*What if...*

19

FREEZE! BUSTED!

I was opening and closing the business and putting in long, 13-hour shifts, often covering for Bob while he had his holidays out of the country with his family. In turn, I always went home at some point in the year. The arrangements worked well for both of us.

I have to say, I loved being a leader and somewhat of a go-to person for the girls on staff. I had never been given such responsibility before.

Whenever Bob went away, I was instructed on what to do and which lawyer to call in case of any trouble. Sure enough, once of the times Bob was away on holiday we were busted. To my credit, and utter amazement, I stayed calm throughout.

I was quite in awe of how it all went down … just like in the movies! Two plain-clothed officers got into the building by pretending to be customers. They looked through the book of photos then, under the pretense of leaving, they held the smoked glass doors wide open and a barrage of uniformed officers ran up the stairs, spilling into the hallway and shouting, 'Freeze!' They continued through the building, shouting loudly, 'POLICE! FREEZE!' as they threw open the doors to the treatment rooms.

Any customers found naked were allowed to get dressed but then had to give their names and addresses before they were let out of the building. The girls' licenses were checked, to ensure that they were all of legal age.

Before we left to be taken downtown, I called out to the girls, telling them not to worry, that I would call the lawyer and get them out. Staff were given the following instructions when they were hired: *If you speak up about how we operate here, you will not have a job to come back to. You will be known as a snitch and be unable to find a job in this same line of work anywhere in the city. But if you say nothing other than your name, and ask for a lawyer, then that lawyer will be provided and paid for by Bob.*

Bob's lawyer got everyone but me released that same day. As I was listed as the manager on the business license, I was kept overnight. Signing the document that made me the official licensee was just one more piece of paper I signed when bob instructed me to do so. I never questioned Bob about anything that was laid in front of me that required my signature, He would say, 'Just sign it, It's legal stuff. You wouldn't understand.' So I just signed it, assuming that Bob would always have my best interests at heart.

Every Christmas, I was given a bonus for putting the business license in my name. Bob explained that this technicality was no big deal. I learned, after getting busted, that indeed, it was a big deal. This is why I spent a horrible, disgusting night in a stinky, cold cell. I was scared to even sit down, everything in the cell was so filthy.

(I was told that if I was busted a second time, the city could deport me as I wasn't a Canadian citizen. I found out that Bob had been busted before and that is why he paid me a bonus to have the license in my name. Bob said this would prevent him from possibly being deported and to justify my yearly bonus. To gain citizenship, I would only have to fill out some forms and take a simple test. That was all that would be required for me to become a Canadian citizen. Again, he discounted the significance of it all with, 'It's no big deal.' However, just a mention of a test scared the hell out of me. I knew my capabilities regarding any kind of studying. Bob picked up the study materials and he quizzed me every day. The day arrived. I am proud to say I passed with flying colours.)

Upon returning to the office after being released from the cells the following day, I was shocked to see the mess the cops had made. Every part of the place had been turned upside down.

Bob returned from his holiday the very next day and we discussed the charges that had been laid against me, and against him. The story soon leaked out to the media. Local television people began phoning and asking for interviews. Then, they gathered at the top of the stairs, trying to gain entry — which was impossible unless they were let in through the buzzer system. Bob asked me to go out and ask them to leave the building.

I firmly asked them to get the camera out of my face, and to leave the area. Once they did that, I locked the outside door. The evening news showed footage of me with my hand in front of the camera asking them to get it out of my face and to leave.

News travels fast! That evening, Richard, who just happened to be back in town visiting his wife's family, called me. 'What the fuck are you doing?' he shouted. He had seen the evening news and was shocked to see where I was working. I cannot say that I blamed him. I was a universe away from the teenager he had married.

Bob and I put our heads together to fight the charges against us. I stood by him 100 percent through all of it, agreeing to say whatever was necessary to keep us both out of trouble.

Bob and I received our court dates. We lost sleep going over what to say and what to do – in the end, we took the advice of our lawyers to answer questions as they came to us, whilst not incriminating ourselves.

After weeks back and forth to our lawyers, none of our charges went to trial. We pled guilty and paid the fines or, I should say, Bob paid the fines. Our story was written about in the newspaper – with full names and full charges spelled out for the world to see. *Charge #1 – Running a common bawdy house. Charge #2 – Living off the avails of prostitution.* My family in Canada washed their hands of me, all except my one auntie that I visited regularly.

In defending us, especially the girls who worked with us, I was in a state of denial. I had thought it was a safe place to work as opposed to being on the street or being controlled by a mean pimp. No one underage was ever hired, everyone was fully licensed with the city, and the staff kept all their own tips.

That kind of business has gone on for many, many years and will go on until the end of time because men will always want to spend time with beautiful women, with no strings attached. If those woman wanted to be there, which all of them did, then why should it be illegal? Several of the girls were putting themselves through school or university and it was their income through the massage parlour that enabled them to do so. However, whether those women would be working in that type of work if there was equally lucrative options was, of course, debatable.

Of course, there were always those few who wanted more and would venture out beyond what the business allowed them. They had a hunger for the fast lane, which Bob always warned, '… will eat you up! Stay away from the fast lane!' As much as Bob liked making money, he believed that pursuing the almighty dollar by going to work in full-service establishments, getting into S & M, or other kinky stuff with other women, was just not worth it.

I always took my job seriously, always remembered the lessons taught to me by life, and by Bob. After forty years in the business, I have so many stories, some good and some bad, some weird and some funny, and many of them quite sad. I always tried to put myself in the shoes of others and be as fair as I could be in any disagreement between the girls, or between one of them and a customer.

I tried and, for the most part, succeeded in not partying with the girls, which they so often did together. I did that so I would not be in a difficult spot if I ever had to reprimand or fire one of them. On one occasion prior to learning that lesson, I had thrown a house party and one of the girls thought it funny to spike my drinks. The day after was the only day I was unable to open shop because I was unbelievably hung over — which was highly unusual for me as I rarely suffered from hangovers.

Over the following years, after Bob had given up doing the training sessions as part of a new arrangement with me, I became the one who personally hired, fired, and trained the girls. As a result, I met many people who are forever imprinted in my memory, along with their stories of the personal journeys that brought them to our business.

In later years, Bob began to buy properties and rent them out to staff. I was no different in that respect, and rented the main floor of a two-story house from Bob. One of my staff members rented the second floor. Later, Bob bought a house closer to the office for me to live in. This was never a mansion of any sort and it certainly was on a seedy street. With some new wallpaper and a slap of paint, it became liveable. Even though I was not paying rent, I was now available 24/7 to sort any problems that arose at work. In hindsight, a move that served Bob more than it did me.

20

MAM, I'M PREGNANT

Bob had taken to visiting me at home prior to work, often catching me in a state of undress. Everyone had routines and I was no different. Bob calculated what time I would return to my home from taking my son to school, then he would arrive there almost to the second. I really didn't feel that denying Bob sex was an option. Luckily, it was always over quickly as his issue of pre-ejaculation was a well-known fact to me. I felt it just wasn't worth the argument. He would claim that this only happened with me because I turned him on instantly. We would leave shortly afterwards in separate cars and meet up for our usual breakfast at the restaurant across the street from the office.

One morning, all the staff had come in and things were running smoothly when a phone call came from my doctor.

'Are you sitting down?' he asked.

'Yes,' I replied.

'Your tests have come back positive for pregnancy. Congratulations!'

Shock! Silence! Then tears … a lot of joyful tears.

I composed myself and called my mum. She was as ecstatic as I was.

Bob, on the other hand, was not! The first words out of his mouth were, 'You have to have an abortion.'

'Absolutely not!' I said. 'Never!'

The next few days were hell. Bob tried to make me feel stupid for even considering going through with the pregnancy. The many discussions about my situation brought out a side of Bob that was all new to me. He was firm in his decision that I terminate my pregnancy; I was just as adamant in my decision to have the baby. Whenever we were together in the office, the atmosphere could have been cut with a knife.

Unfortunately for me, it was not long before it all ended abruptly.

One day, I went to the hospital doubled over in pain. Later, I woke up in a ward where I was told by the doctor that my tests were still showing I was pregnant, but that I had suffered a ruptured ovarian cyst. I spent six days in hospital and then went back to work, spending most of my time sitting behind the desk. As I healed from my six-inch incision, I forced a smile on my face for customers, and continued to listen to Bob's unrelenting, pathetic attempts to convince me not to go through with the pregnancy.

Over the next week, instead of gradually going away, my

pain only increased, to the point that I found it difficult to walk. My doctor was on holidays so I made an appointment to see the doctor who was looking after his patients. He happened to be a specialist in gynecology. After an examination, he told me that my pregnancy was ectopic, that my baby was blocked in the fallopian tube and would soon die. He went on to say that this condition was dangerous for my life and so the baby must be removed as soon as possible. He would make the arrangements for me to go straight to the hospital. I was more than devasted.

It took a while to get over my loss, and the pain of that second incision so soon after the first. Bob tried to give his sympathies but I knew they were not heartfelt. They meant nothing to me. I grieved for my unborn child, but I kept my sadness and tears to myself. There was only a handful of people close enough to me that knew what I was going through.

After the loss of my baby, I became obsessed with becoming a mother, one way or another. I checked out a procedure called in vitro fertilization (IVF), which involves combining donor sperm and my eggs in a laboratory. Then, once one or more embryos form, they are placed in the uterus. It was very expensive and only done in an adjacent province, which added to the horrendous cost of the procedure.

My assistant manager knew my plight. As time passed, we talked about the ridiculous amount of money it would cost for an IVF. Now in the mid '80s, IVF was a very new and costly procedure, with no guarantee of success. We joked that maybe it could be done just as easily with a turkey baster and save all that money. Crazy talk!

After many hours of tears and talking through what

had happened to me, the subject of surrogacy came up in a more serious way. She said she would be willing to be a surrogate for me.

Her husband was away at the time, for what reason I cannot remember. It was a normal thing for some of the girls to be working at a place like ours while their partners were in the army or working out of town. I was ecstatic about the prospect of surrogacy. Bob was with us during one of those chats about the surrogacy process. Now with him having more understanding that this could become real, he listened more intently. The conversation drifted to the topic of who the father would be.

'Oh,' my assistant said. 'I thought that because you two are an item that it would be Bob.'

It only took mere seconds for Bob to volunteer his 'services.' I questioned why Bob was so gung ho on being part of this process, when he was so opposed to my earlier pregnancy. It crossed my mind that being involved turned him on in some strange way. I entertained another possible reason – that he genuinely felt for me because I had lost my baby. The last possible reason that crossed my mind was that he wanted to be involved so that he would always have a connection to me.

He could have just wanted to have sex with her to add another notch to his belt. He was well known for adding to that long list. But then, I was certainly no innocent, the difference being that I was single. At that time, he and I were alike in our crazy sex lives, having rendezvous together with multiple partners was a regular thing. In that sense, we were connected at the hip. I often wondered what he told his wife, especially when he went home late, stinking of booze.

One night after work, he and I were out at a bar when my phone rang. It was my assistant manager calling to tell me we should come to the office after closing because she was ovulating.

'No problem!' I told her excitedly.

On the way to the office, Bob asked, 'How does she know that she is ovulating?'

'Through body temperature,' I said. 'Plus, she has three kids … she knows … that's all I care about.'

The subsequent experience was nothing like Bob had expected it to be. It took all of two minutes and was over and done. I was right there beside them, orchestrating the whole thing. From a standing position, I got in between them, enticed Bob into an erection, and then manoeuvred him into place for the final act from behind. They came together only as far as necessary to do the deed. Afterwards, he was angry and said he would never do that again. Then, he went down the hall, saying he had to use the toilet. He was pissed off, having anticipated something more than the quick, passionless moment that hadn't even been a proper threesome!

A couple of weeks later, my assistant announced to us both that she was pregnant. Bob was in denial. He said it was impossible to know for certain so soon. I, on the other hand, took her word for it and was just beaming with joy, saying that it happened so easily because it was meant to be, that it was a pure miracle.

When it was confirmed, Bob started to panic. He made me promise never to tell anyone that he was the father.

At the time, Bob's nephew from the Caribbean was visiting. He said he wanted to find a wife and stay in the country.

I knew that my adoption of the baby would go through more easily if I was married. I knew him from visiting his country with Bob and found him to be very handsome. He was ten years younger than me, but that didn't matter to either of us. Bob was all for it. The marriage took place and my new husband moved into my house. Unfortunately, it turned out to be a complete disaster and our marriage was never consummated. (He stayed with me at the house on and off until the adoption went through, then returned to his home country.)

It was not long before my assistant manager started showing a baby bump. I took her to her doctor appointments whenever I could. I listened to the doctor's advice and read about what she was supposed to do as a pregnant woman. I made sure she had the right food for the right month, and constantly wanted to feel her belly when the baby was kicking.

I went over and over in my mind what this little one's name would be. If it was a boy, he would have this name, and if a girl, she would have that name … or maybe this other one. I changed the names around in my mind constantly.

21

WELCOME TO MY LIFE

Finally, the phone call came. She had gone into labour. I called Bob and said I was leaving the desk and going to the hospital. I rushed, of course, even arriving before her. Immediately, I panicked because she was not there. I called her.

'Where are you?'

Nonchalantly, she announced that she had stopped at McDonald's for something to eat.

'Who does that?' I thought.

Before long we were all in the delivery room. Everyone there knew the situation. I was going to be the mother of this beautiful baby through private adoption. Everyone was so kind, encouraging me to be right there at every moment of the birth so I would not miss a thing.

I was concerned about my assistant because she was not making a sound throughout. I had thought screaming and cursing were all part of giving birth. I kept wiping her forehead and asking if she needed anything. She kept pushing the oxygen mask into her face hard and taking deep breaths. I'm sure she wanted me to just leave her alone.

Then, the doctor called out, 'It's a boy!' and bundled him. Within a minute or so, my tiny baby was handed to me. I was sobbing as I took him, holding him to my chest. As I looked down at him, I immediately thought my life as I once knew it was going to change forever. I took my baby to the farthest corner of the room and, through my tears, I told him that I finally knew what life was all about. I promised him that I would never stop loving him as long as I had breath in my body.

My aunt, the only relative who was speaking to me at the time and, through my tears, I told her my son had arrived and how beautiful he was. 'It's just sad,' I said, 'that no one is here to share my joy.' My aunt joined me at the hospital that evening my son was born, and we drooled over him together. I had settled on his name, which was as perfect as he was. I stayed overnight with him; the next day, I took in all that a nurse showed me about his bathing and feeding. I was in heaven!

My assistant was wheeled back to her room. I asked after her wellbeing over the next couple of days, but I never saw her again until she passed my baby over the threshold of the hospital doors to me – one of the quirky rules of adoption at the time. My son's face was covered throughout that entire time so she would never see him. By mutual agreement, my assistant manager was planning to take her children and move to a different province immediately after the birth, where she would meet up with her husband when he was able.

I never saw her again. It was agreed that we would not contact each other in the future. I always wanted to be truthful with my son about how he had come to be. When he was older, around ten or twelve years, we tried to find his birth mother but, sad to say, we never did. Every lead I had was a dead end. I was willing to break the agreement regardless of the consequences, to carry out my son's wishes.

One of the nurses gave me a hand-written poem, which I still cherish:

> *Not flesh of my flesh*
> *Not bone of my bone*
> *Never forget*
> *For a single minute*
> *You never grew under my heart,*
> *But in it.*

Once again, I started to re-evaluate my life. I realized how much control Bob had over me. My job was work, sleep, and Bob. I had no friends, just work colleagues, most of the staff were out for themselves and it was a fact — no one likes the boss. Especially with all the rules that I had to enforce. No this was not your regular 9 to 5. Bob was against my having friends outside of work – one of the reasons was that he assumed any friends I might have would likely encourage me to go out to party. How could I possibly go out with coworkers as friends, and then maybe have to reprimand them for some sort of bad behaviour at work? 'You are not one of the girls anymore. You are their boss,' he would say. I would like to think that I was fair with all my staff, but I'm sure there were feathers ruffled somewhere.

When it was time to leave the hospital, Bob saw his son for the first time. He sat with him on his lap in the entrance, staring intently into my son's eyes.

22

I TOLD YOU THAT I WILL
MAKE YOU LOVE ME

As much as my son meant a 180-degree turn around in lifestyle for me, I loved being a mum. Bob visited daily, generally for an hour each time, and it soon became clear that he loved his new son as much as I did. But all too soon, babysitters were in place, and it was time to go back to work. The only difference in my work load was there were no more double shifts for me – I had a baby to go home to. I decided to work the evening shift which was 6 p.m. until 12 midnight. I felt those were the hours that my son would be asleep in bed. That meant that I would be with him during the day and could see so much more of his daily growth and achievements. I had hired a staff member for the job, so I knew her well and she was used to working those crazy hours.

Back at work, I soon discovered Bob was up to his old tricks, flirting with staff members. He always argued that it was part of the role he had to play so that he could get them on his side for the sake of the business. They would be more likely to open up to him and talk about anyone else who might be breaking rules, such as giving full service for larger tips, or stealing his customers by dating them outside the business, therefore eliminating desk fees.

Often the girls that walked through those smoke glass doors, just as I had done years earlier, had hit rock bottom. Most of the time, their self-esteem was at its lowest. It was all too easy for Bob to turn on the charm and have new girls falling for his bullshit. I talked to him about his behaviour many times but could not make him understand how hurt the girls were when they realised that they weren't as special as he tried to make them feel. I asked myself the question: why did I care? Was I jealous? Bob knew exactly what he was doing and he wasn't going to change; it was me who was the stupid one. Now that I wasn't spending as many hours with Bob, it wasn't long before I found out from gossiping staff that he was receiving blow jobs. I told myself that I didn't give a damn but when one of his conquests was my babysitter, it made me more than angry.

I convinced myself that I did not care, but I never succeeded. In fact, it was never more obvious that Bob had hurt my feelings. He had bragged that he would one day make me love him and, apparently, he had succeeded.

I cried many times wanting my life to be different. The work I was involved in didn't make me feel good about myself in any way. Now my position had turned around and I was the one teaching these young girls how to bathe naked men, teaching them to take all emotion out of what they were doing, telling them to compare their work to something as stupid as washing windows. Everything was de-personalized. In the staff room, new girls were told by other attendants, 'If you choose to give blow jobs, just pretend you're sucking on a banana.'

While my son was still young, Bob sometimes took his wife and growing family of two sons back to his homeland to visit. My role changed yet again to accommodate Bob – not only looking after the business, but looking after the family dog. I managed the business, doing payroll, banking, picking up supplies, and everything he would have been doing for the business if he was not away on holidays. There were always many tasks to deal with, such as driving new girls to get their license, taking photos of staff for the client albums, buying and selling uniforms, doing schedules, dealing with difficult customers and staff, checking lockers for illicit booze and drugs. It was the fast lane and it was busy, busy, busy. I managed all the challenges of the place well, perhaps too well because it began to dawn on me that Bob cared more for my work ethic, my reliability, and my obsessive/compulsive tendencies in keeping the place clean than he did about me.

Occasionally, one of the girls would point out this disparity. 'I see what you have and what he has, and yet you're giving him your life.' I talked to Bob about my financial situation and worries about money in the future. Now that I was a mother, there was more than just me to be concerned about. He only responded with, 'Don't worry, you two will always be looked after.'

Such comments stuck in my mind. It was helpful to know that my sacrifice, so to speak, would be worth it. At times when I felt that I just couldn't deal with Bob's bullshit any further, that I had reached a breaking point, it would be holiday time once more. This meant bonus time which was paid to me for having the city license in my name. My wage never seemed to go up, but my bonus did. The years passed and by 2020, my bonus had been raised up to $20,000. The bonus renewed my commitment and energies, as these funds enabled me to travel back and forth to England. Bob was the ultimate controller. He knew all the tricks that worked.

I lived the pretense of being in a different type of work every time we visited family in England. I told myself that my son and I were living the best life. I spent my bonus on trips home and creating a beautiful holiday. My family in the UK were always thrilled to see us, we had so much fun.

With an eye to my family's future, I bought two life insurance policies, making my son the beneficiary. I was able to buy my mum's home, a council house, from the local government. Every time I went home, I fixed something or bought new things that I knew would make her life easier. I also began investing in the stock market, which turned into a favourite pastime, buying and selling stocks on my own until I decided to get a broker.

Bob had his own broker. Predictably — a female broker. From the beginning of their relationship, I felt that there was more than just business meetings happening. I had accepted that some things, many things, were not worth the drama, or the trauma. I was slowly coming to the realization that I would never be able to change who Bob really was. I felt I had to accept my life's choices.

I always suspected … now, I knew … that Bob messed around with the girls who worked for him. He had even more freedom to do so than he had before my son's birth. Our girls were very pretty playboy/playgirl material so I justified to myself that any man in Bob's shoes would take advantage of such a situation. He was like a child in a candy store. We had 25-30 girls working at the parlour. We were never short staffed. Girls just wanted to work with us because they knew, via the grapevine, that we were busy and that the girls were not allowed to give Full Service.

My son made me so happy! And my job, which unfortunately, included my relationship with Bob, enabled me to spoil my son. As he grew, we joined all types of extracurricular activities, such as computer classes, swimming, and music lessons. I was thrilled with being a mum and, alas, it was my job that enabled my lifestyle.

Occasionally, Bob would say, 'You need someone to love. Someone to love you back and always something to look forward to.'

To his credit, Bob dedicated at least an hour of his day to our son, whether it was joining us for a McDonald's meal or play-fighting with him at home. My son called him uncle and whenever Bob left, he cried and pleaded for him to stay longer. Bob had bought some lake-front property and went there most weekends with his two boys. So when he was away for these days in a row, our son's crying episodes got worse. He was heartbroken.

23

DENY DENY DENY

My son and I always had a great time visiting my family back in England. It was like going into a different world, a world of normality for both of us. When we returned, he went back to school, and I went back to work.

After one such trip, I immediately sensed something had happened with one of the girls. It was a gut feeling, but it turned out to be a story that sent shivers up and down my spine.

She was a pretty Mexican girl who was married at the time, but her husband was in the army and away on deployment. She came forward and said she would need some time off because she was pregnant. She went on to say that she needed to have an abortion. When I asked her who was the father, she told me that because of her lifestyle with all the crazy partying, she had no idea who it could be.

When I left the office that day on my way to pick up my son from school, a feeling came over me that I could not shake. The nervous glances I saw between my boss and the cute Mexican while she was telling us the story in the office kept flashing through my mind. I decided to pay her a visit at home early the next morning before opening the parlour.

To say she was surprised to see me would have been an understatement because that sort of thing just was not done in our business. It was totally out of the ordinary.

She answered the door and then said, 'Oh, hi,' and then nervously invited me in.

'I need to talk to you, I need to ask you a question.'

'Sure, what is it? Sit down.'

Then, I began my speech that I had repeated to myself while driving over to her home. I had even said it out loud to practise being as convincing as I could. 'Bob asked me to come here. We both want to know if you would be willing to follow through with the pregnancy so that my son could have a brother or sister by the same father? Bob is fully on board with the idea,' I lied.

Her response came quickly. There was no denial of actually sleeping with Bob. 'No, no,' she said, in a panicked voice. 'I couldn't do that! The child would be born after my husband's return from the army. I must get rid of the baby before he comes back.'

Then, I confessed that the boss had not sent me.

'I came here only because I had a gut feeling. Get him on the phone,' I said.

She did as I asked and then, from across the room, I could hear him shouting at her.

'Just deny, deny, deny! How can you be so stupid?'

'It's too late,' she said to him in tears. 'She knows!'

The world around me slowed. Their voices became muted. A few moments later, in a trance-like state, I quietly let myself out while they were still on the phone. I did not know how to feel or what to say or do.

I wondered how I ever got into such a situation. I was supposedly the girlfriend of a married man but not only was he cheating on his wife constantly with me, but he was cheating on me as well. I felt guilty for thinking I could love such a man. I questioned the reasons why Bob wanted me in his life, telling me how much he loved me, and then screwing around like a dirty tom cat.

I decided to pick up a few things from the grocery. I certainly was not going to breakfast with Bob. I walked around the store in a foggy mist of anger, not knowing how to deal with any of it. Could I walk away from everything, get a 'job,' and start again.

Stupidly, I found a way to forgive him — mainly because I felt backed into a corner. I always convinced myself that he loved both me and my son, but that sex was so animalistic in our line of business that cheating did not have the same meaning as it did with normal people.

So, I told myself that it was the business that had corrupted him. It certainly was not my fault that he was so promiscuous. I reminded myself that I was the mistress, the 'other woman' in the situation, not the wife. I had no rights to tell him what to do and what not to do.

You had to know him. Only then would you understand how I and many others fell under his controlling ways. I honestly felt sorry for the Mexican girl. She had fallen for the flattery that Bob turned off and on at will to achieve his selfish goal of sleeping with her. It was me who demanded the appointment be brought forward and paid for privately as opposed to the date that was set for later which would have been free thanks to healthcare. I drove her to get the abortion, an act which bothers me to this day.

I decided enough was enough! Even though we had not long been back from England, I returned home and desperately tried to make a go of it there. I enrolled my son in local daycare, put my name forward for government housing, and got a job in a pub.

I told my father that Bob and I had broken up. To say that he was pleased was an understatement. My dad was helpful and encouraging beyond belief. He genuinely wanted things to work out for my son and I. He tried hard to make me see that life would get better, and that I had made the right decision.

Bob kept at me, never letting up on the phone calls, telling me how much he loved me. Every day he would call, telling me that if it wasn't for his children, he would be with me.

Again, I was all too quick to fall for his spiel. Along with the daily phone calls, he began to send heartfelt letters, expressing his feelings of despair and the need for both of us to return to him. I genuinely tried to make things work. I declared myself homeless with the government and was given a temporary flat on a street called Ordnance Lane. It had a disgusting reputation but you had to go through this process to be given a permanent government property. My dad came to help, bringing a bottle of bleach and we scrubbed the place down. I never slept there; I just pretended to sleep there. It was just that disgusting.

My dad drove me to and from my new bar job. Life was harder than I expected and I felt like I had gone back in time. Thanks to my stock market investments crashing, I had no money; I was sofa surfing between my parents' homes, and popping into the disgusting temporary housing that I had been assigned. It was okay until it wasn't. I just gave up.

Unfortunately, I was as obsessed with Bob as he claimed to be with me and my son. I tearfully left my family and returned back to Canada.

I wanted to believe that we were some kind of soulmates captured in a kind of torturous trance for life. We bounced off each other and we could not keep our hands off each other. We both had high sex drives and we both had achieved the ultimate in pure satisfaction every time. I had turned into a one-man woman, but nothing had really changed for him.

My hopes for something better with him, and my resolve to put up with his crap because we loved each other, eventually always weakened. I found myself in the same situation, convincing myself that I stayed so my son could have a better life. I endured so much because of Bob's insecurities, his lust, and his narcissism.

He became very insecure with me. He wanted to know where I was all the time. If he called me on the phone and the line was busy, he demanded to know who I had been talking to. One day, I was driving home from work when he called and asked what I was doing. I told him I had picked up and dropped off supplies and now was on my way home. He laughed and said, 'Look in your rearview mirror. I'm right behind you.' This was one of his tests to see if I would lie to him regarding my whereabouts. I had never given him reason to start thinking the way he did. I put it down to his own insecurities.

Bob was always generous toward us. Business was good and getting better all the time and he was the primary beneficiary, getting wealthier and wealthier as each year passed. At one point, I had to have major surgery and he paid for my friend from England to come and stay with us to help with my son. Another year, I said that I wanted to take my son to Disneyland but had no one to go with. Bob gave my sister and her son an all-expense paid trip to join us — it was a trip of a lifetime from England to Disneyland for them both.

I never told anyone in any detail about my situation with him. I just forced a smile and let everyone think I was living 'the life.' I think my dad was the only person that truly understood. He spelled it out for me in so many ways. He could see, and said so, that I was going down a road to loneliness — and loneliness is the worst emotion anyone ever endures.

He wrote me a letter in November 1987:

Dear Sandra,

I wouldn't be me if I didn't warn you about the kind of life you are letting yourself in for, but being your father and loving you as I do … why don't you find a man of your own or ask Bob to live with you and him be your man? You're a caring person, loyal and loaded with affection. Too much to share a man with another woman. I know you have already made up your mind but if you have ever taken notice of anyone or anything in your life, take notice of what I say. There is no reason I should steer you wrong. Love is the essence of life. It's all about sharing and caring. Everyone wants to be loved and also to return that love. But this only works when there is one man and one woman.

Love Dad
XXXXX

Bob continued to leave for the lake and his cabin most weekends and I would busy myself with monitoring work and encouraging my son's friends to come for sleepovers. The overnights kept him happy which made me happy. Bob started talking about how sad it was that his son could not enjoy the water sports and all the things that went along with owning a lakeside cottage.

24

THE SHERIFF AND THE DEPUTY

~~~

After many more months of this unsettled existence, I started talking once more about going back to England permanently.

'I have a large family so they will help us to settle.'

Bob's reaction to my suggestion of moving back to England was anger, 'You could never support yourself!'

Bob and I decided that Bob would tell his wife about my son — his son — so that possibly, in time, my son would be able to enjoy some of the lifestyle that his other children enjoyed. Bob said he would have to tell her that he had just been the provider of the sperm and that it was all done via IVF, that it was done to help me have a child because I was his right-hand person at work and he wanted to help me.

My son had just turned six years of age when I walked him into Bob's family home. Before this moment, my son called Bob ' Uncle Bob.' My son seemed overjoyed with the news that he finally had someone to call 'Dad.' For the first time ever, I had to put a face to the wife and deal head-on with all the lies. All of the deception and guilt that had accumulated over the years made me feel ill.

Then, the question was asked, what should my son call Bob's wife. I had already given thought to that and had asked that her first name be used in front of the title *Mom*. Bob's family members seemed to come out of the woodwork that day — they all wanted to meet Bob's new son.

I had always kept my son busy with extracurricular activities but soon found myself enrolling him in even more activities as our lives were taken over by Bob and his family. His kids especially would talk directly to my son, saying things like, 'Ask your mum if you can stay for a sleepover.'

Then, they would fill his head with the offers of enticing and exciting things a six year-old would love to do, such as building a life-size wrestling ring, or playing the drums, or swimming in their backyard pool. I couldn't say, 'No,' as my son would be upset. This was all new and exciting to him.

Most of the time, I was able to keep him busy with swimming lessons, Kumon math, and music. Bob, his wife and his sons talked about wanting my son to get into Karate. Both of Bob's sons had trained for years and had received their black belts.

I found myself agreeing after Bob's sons got my son all hyped up, watching the movie, *The Karate Kid*. It was agreed that I should enroll him in karate lessons three times a week. I suddenly found myself sharing the audience at Karate with the wife.

I talked to Bob about the whole family takeover, not in so many words, but in terms of what I was feeling. I said it was not supposed to be like that. It was supposed to be just an odd weekend away at the lake so that our son could enjoy the cabin and water sports with your family. His response was that 'our' son was happy enjoying his family, especially his brothers and cousins. Many times, after Bob's sons would encourage him to stay for sleepovers, I would make the drive back home alone, with tears rolling down my cheeks, wondering what I had done. I was certain they were trying to take him away from me.

I was invited to go to the lake with them. I found myself alongside the wife in the kitchen helping prepare meals or doing other mundane jobs. Bob had little to say to me when his wife was around. I felt he was scared to speak. If I was invited to Bob's house, I found myself doing the same things as I did at the lake, busying myself in the kitchen, trying to be a part of the family. But mostly I felt like a mistrusted intruder, or a piece of furniture.

The wife liked to think she was in charge — and she was in charge of the home and the meals, but that was the extent of her realm. Otherwise, Bob was king. Many times, I witnessed him being treated like royalty, his favourite drink always poured for him upon his arrival, dinner always served to him as he sat down in his own special chair.

I don't think the wife had any idea who she was married to, or who he really was after he walked out the front door of their home. In fact, I know she had been told never to even ask about his work and its issues. He told me that he provided his family's lifestyle and that was all his wife needed to know.

On one visit to their home, Bob's wife asked me to go into the back room and talk with her or, rather, to listen to her. I felt cornered. I always felt guilty around her. I had no option but to sit and listen. She told me that her sister had told her that Bob and I had gone off to Vegas — that she was fully aware of that trip because her sister worked in the travel business. I told her that a bunch of girls had gone on the trip, which was true.

That trip had been one of many, including a trip to Trinidad, which had happened prior to my son's birth. She was suspicious, and rightly so. She made it clear that from that day forward all she wanted from me was honesty.

She said she and Bob had a very good sex life and a very good marriage and that 'all of this' could work. I felt compelled to tell her I was just one of several girls on that trip to Vegas, just part of the group. I wanted to tell her that I was also one of several women that Bob was screwing around with but, of course, I didn't.

Bob continued to visit my home after he finished work to play with my son. He even kept a set of track bottoms and a t-shirt in the closet so he could change from his office attire and freely wrestle with my son on the floor. My son loved that.

One evening, after my son had had his play time and bath time and was settled in for the night, Bob and I were sitting having a night cap at the kitchen table. His wife walked in the front door and angrily asked what was going on. I thought that she was okay with the situation. Bob calmly explained that he had just stopped by to say goodnight. He offered a few other plausible excuses for being there, but finally, he just threw his hands up and pointed to each of us in turn, saying, 'I love you, and I love you ... so you two figure it out.' Then, he walked out and, having nothing to say to me, she promptly followed.

Normally, I am a deep thinker, a wallflower, a people watcher. The way I consoled myself for having fallen in love with that man was to believe that if it wasn't me, it would have been someone else. He had long ago made it one of his life's passions to have at least one regular 'outside' woman. I was his choice. In the early years, he was not my choice but I realised I cared for him more and more as time passed due to the genuine love he had for our son.

One night, when my son was away having a sleepover at his stepmom's house, Bob arranged a small get-together for a visiting friend from his home country. It was to take place at my apartment. Bob made sure that all the food was ordered and coming. Most of the food was catered in by another friend of Bob's who owned a very successful restaurant. He ('Mr Caterer') and his very young, very beautiful girlfriend showed up, carrying containers of succulent lobster.

The party was still going strong at 3 a.m. when Bob had to leave, along with Mr. Caterer. Bob tried to encourage his friend to leave as well but the friend did not want to. Bob could not order him to do so. It was obvious the guy was still in the mood to party.

Bob gave me instructions to try to tone it down and call it a night as soon as possible. I did my best by playing some sombre music but, to my surprise, Mr. Caterer's girlfriend started doing a very sensual strip dance to that music.

All the while, I was having a deep conversation with Bob's friend, who soon made it clear to me that he was anxious to spell out just how stupid I was for giving my life to 'that' man. I was taken aback by what he was telling me as I thought this man was Bob's friend. I told him it was not just about me, that Bob paid for my son's private schooling and was going to put him through university. I went on to say that Bob's place of work was my livelihood, and he helped me when I was at my lowest point in life.

I was in shock when he replied that he would pay for my son's university, that there was no need for such a beautiful person as me to give up my life in such a way. I told him it was too late for me to consider accepting any such offer because I was in love with Bob, not to mention the fact that my son's life would be in total upheaval if he was pulled away from his father and now, his new siblings. I was not going to put him through that.

I felt strongly that it was all booze talk, but he boldly told me some things that I had not known. He said that in his home country, almost every man of wealth had an outside woman. The wife is called the *sheriff* and the outside woman is called the *deputy*.

Meanwhile, the strip tease was still happening. She probably thought she was being ignored, and had now moved herself into position on the arm of the couch next to Bob's friend. The next move she made was to wrap her naked legs around his neck from behind him. It was time for me to show them where they could sleep ... or whatever.

The next morning when the house was still quiet and

Bob's wealthy friend and I were sitting alone drinking our morning coffee, he continued talking about paying for my son's education. Suddenly, Bob appeared at the top of the stairs looking perturbed. Luckily, I had heard him let himself in and stopped the conversation with my index finger across my mouth.

Bob came to the table with a huge bag of breakfast goodies from McDonald's. Once he was satisfied that it was not me who had slept with his wealthy friend, his demeanor returned to normal and he started telling us how his friend, Mr. Caterer, who had left the party with him, was paranoid about having to leave his girlfriend behind at my place because she was drunk and apt to start strip dancing.

Mr. Wealthy apologized to Bob, asking how he could possibly have said no to that beautiful pussy staring him in the face. 'I'm sorry,' he said with a laugh, 'but it had to be done.'

Just then the phone rang. It was the Mr. Caterer wanting to know if his girlfriend was still there.

'Yes,' I said. 'She is still sleeping.'

Mr. Wealthy suggested I say that I had shared the bed with Mr. Caterer's girlfriend, not him. Before Mr. Caterer showed up, I went into the bedroom to convince the 20-year-old of what she should say. Incoherently, she agreed, rolled over and went back to sleep.

Soon after, Mr. Caterer walked in. He looked around and not seeing his girlfriend, asked where she was. I pointed at the door and he went into the room where she was sleeping. We could hear him calling to her and attempting to shake her awake. When he got no response from her, he joined us at the table where I told him that I had shared the bed with her and Mr.

Wealthy had slept in the spare room.

Mr. Caterer went back into the bedroom to try again to wake her. He was soon back staring at me with a face like thunder. She had bluntly told him that she had had wild, all-night sex with Mr. Wealthy. Mr. Caterer walked out without saying a word to any of us.

I was left feeling like a big liar. Mr. Wealthy apologized to me, and everyone went their separate ways while I tidied up. Mr. Caterer did not speak to me again for many years because of the lies I had told him that night.

Close to the end of his holiday, Mr. Wealthy decided he wanted to take us all out for a fancy dinner prior to his departure, as a thank-you for everyone's hospitality. The dinner guests included Bob, the wife and her two sons, my son and me. It became very clear to me that everyone in Bob's life had a particular role, and mine was to provide him with personal 'fun.'

I didn't meet Mr. Wealthy again until my next visit to Bob's home country when he was shocked to find out that Bob and I were still together after so many years. He openly told me — in front of Bob — that if I ever needed him ... if Bob was not looking out for me, to just call him, to just tell him, and he would sort Bob out. Yet, I never had his phone number, nor was I offered it. I put this down to bullshit talk on his part. I am certainly not sure why a supposed friend of Bob's would so badly want me to leave his friend. It crossed my mind that maybe it had been a setup designed by Bob to discover if I had any private intentions that Bob did not know about, after all the two men were supposed to be close friends. I had learned to be suspicious of everything that came from Bob or anyone associated with him.

Many times, I have wanted to reach out for some help to escape my sordid life, but I always feared the consequences. Jokes were passed around easily with lots of laughter between Bob and his business associates about how easy it was to get rid of someone who was giving you problems, 'especially in the old country.' When Bob got into business with a loud Russian man, the guy would tell stories about how it was no problem to make someone disappear.

I am sure the stories were told in front of me to keep me in check and to let me know how powerful men with money were.

25

BOB THE SPY

Finally, I thought I had come up with the perfect solution to my life situation — and it did not entail getting on a plane to England. I talked to Bob about it, and to my surprise, he agreed that I should have the freedom to come and go as I pleased. He also agreed that I should find a partner. I suggested that if that happened, I would always fool around with Bob on the side.

This arrangement might sound a bit bizarre to 'normal' people, but to me it was a way of changing my life so that both my son and I could be happy. I hoped that including an ongoing commitment to him would allow him to see how unfair the current situation was for me. We also discussed how I would still be able to work and make a living, and that my son would still be a large part of his family's life.

If he didn't agree to my plan, I was going to go home

to England and take my son with me. 'I cannot live like this anymore,' I told him.

After hearing my teary plea, to my great surprise, he agreed. I immediately started hanging out with different staff members, testing the waters of my new found freedom. The girls at work started to open up to me more when they realized that I was no longer running to the boss to tell him every little thing that happened or that I had heard. I was becoming their confidant. I expanded my freedom to making decisions as to where I went, even traveling across the border a couple of times with my son where we stayed in a hotel with an outdoor pool.

Bob had been very agreeable and I wondered if he was just appeasing me short term. I'm sure that he was thinking to himself that he could easily reel me back into place.

One day, after putting my son to bed, I was talking on the phone with a co-worker who I had befriended. I saw something shiny underneath the bedside table. The person I was talking to was telling me in confidence about certain customers she was seeing outside the business in order to make extra money.

I reached down and pulled the shiny thing forward. It was connected to my phone.

'Oh shit!' I said. 'It's a tape recorder!'

My coworker, started yelling, 'How could he get into your place? I thought he had returned his key! How could he do this to you...'

I was speechless.

'I am going to lose my job,' she screamed. 'This must be illegal! Call the police.'

I told her the device probably came from one of his cop

friends and, aside from that, I reminded her, 'Don't forget he is my son's father. I just cannot call the police on him.'

As it happened, the recorder had not been set up properly. After fiddling around with it, I realized it had just recorded a bunch of high-pitched squeals.

However, that did not take away from the fact that Bob had never really accepted my plea for freedom.

When I confronted him with the recording device, he made it loud and clear that my getting out meant losing everything, and always making a point of asking how I would ever support myself and my son. 'Everybody in this town knows you are my girlfriend, except for you!' he yelled at me.

I cannot defend the relationship, nor am I proud of it. I felt very strongly over the years that the wife, especially in earlier times, chose to look the other way. I do not think she could ever stand up and truthfully say that she did not know about Bob and me. I think she was as much controlled by him as I was. I found myself often feeling sorry for her and thinking that I wouldn't want to swap positions with the Sherriff. She always presented such a loving personality toward my son and courtesy towards me. However, I always sensed an undercurrent of jealousy and resentment when I was in her presence. I, in turn, was feeling a huge amount of guilt.

If Bob was always awful to me it would have been easier to leave. But along with all the negatives, there were and continued to be fabulous times with him. The belly laughs with the family were in abundance. I accepted that I had to try to be happy, especially around my son. I got very good at painting a smile on my face.

26

FANTASY LAND

Always looking for new opportunities to make even more money, Bob became extremely successful over the years. He often told me I should also put some of my earnings away but there never seemed to be enough to go around, especially when it came to keeping up with the spending habits of the rest of the family. In fact, I became quite despondent with the whole notion of saving and investing. I found it difficult to keep my head above water regarding bills, but I just had to leave at Christmas, or go away somewhere with just my son. My yearly bonus in December barely covered my debt load of the previous year. I was always playing catch up. My total cheque and bonus money never seemed to be enough. Bob often reminded me that I had no mortgage to pay and that he paid for the fancy dinners when we went out. He calculated that I was making $100,000 a year if I was to take those things into consideration. This might be true, it was my trips away and these escapes that were killing me financially. I always tried to give my son a holiday of a lifetime every year, whether it was to Vancouver to visit my brother or across the water to see my side of the family.

I felt many times that stress would be my demise, that along with the fact that I had been diagnosed with PFO (*patent foramen ovale*) which is a small hole in the wall that separates the heart's upper chambers. It occurs when the opening doesn't close after birth. The hole had been repaired with a simple stent inserted through my groin. Of course, having been a smoker since the age of ten or earlier, was not the way to live with a heart defect of any kind.

One of Bob's investments was in the hotel business. The hotel he invested in not only housed a popular strip joint; it was also well known for its problems with gangs. He made it his goal to clean it up. When he suggested that my 16-year-old son should work there at the beer vending desk with his half-brother, I refused to let him. Bob thought it was safe enough - Bob's sons were ten or more years older than my son, adults, plus there were bouncers that worked at the club. Still I refused.

Bob had rebuilt his cottage at the lake. Before the work had begun, he was always talking about the plans. One day, while showing his wife and me the blueprints, he noted that the bedrooms were going to have adjoining doors so that we three could sleep together and then return to our own beds. Because I had been with Bob in the early years of the business when we used to have threesomes and foursomes, I knew this was a turn-on fantasy of his. He was not joking. He had dropped too many casual hints and innuendos.

But with his wife involved ... that would be a whole different ball game, certainly not something I wanted in the slightest. But I knew that his off-the-cuff remark, pretending to be joking, was his way of starting a plan. He never did anything without long-term planning and this one was under way ... I had seen it before. This one would bring his biggest fantasy to life.

It wasn't long before he took the next step to try and make his fantasy become a reality. I stayed over one night because it was not safe for me to drive home. All of us had had a lot to drink because it was someone's birthday. I was asleep with my son when Bob woke me up to ask if I would come to their bed because his wife had requested it.

'Are you nuts?' I said. 'What if the kids wake up? No way! Leave me alone!'

He left the room but came back a second time to try to convince me. I still refused and, thankfully, that night was never spoken about again. I even questioned myself, wondering if I had dreamt it or had it really happened? Did the wife even know? I tried to visualize him telling her to be quiet and enjoy it because I, in a drunken stupor, had supposedly stumbled into their bed by mistake. Our previous experimenting with threesomes or foursomes had never been a regular thing and had stopped altogether after my son was born. It fulfilled his fantasy but never mine. I went along only if it was with women I did not know on a personal level. As well, I always made sure to be good and drunk to enable me to give him his fantasy. I long ago discovered that the sober me was often very different from the drunk, party person hidden away inside.

When my son finished his private schooling at sixteen, his dad bought him a new car. It was sitting in Bob's driveway when we pulled up outside his home. The whole family was waiting to celebrate. The shiny, new car had a huge red bow tied around it. I was so happy for my son. He was just so pleased.

I had been manipulated for years. I was sure it had been a plan on Bob's part from Day One. The sad thing is that I was the one that let it happen because I wanted my son to have a better life than what I could give him without Bob's help. It had happened again that day with the new car. I felt the same as I did when driving away from leaving my son for sleepovers. How could I compete with this? With the gifts? Of course, it wasn't the kids fault, they had no idea. They just loved each other sincerely and my son loved them back. I thought it was one of the only beautiful things that came from this whole saga.

I had convinced Bob to let me go home to England and spend some time with my ailing Mum. My dad had already died from lung cancer and I had taken my son home for his funeral. I felt guilty about missing so much of my dad's life once he became sober. I truly loved him. When my mum was diagnosed with Alzheimer's, I planned with Bob to let my son stay at his home with his boys as I wasn't sure how long I was going to be away. I didn't want my son to miss the start of university. He was excited to move in with his dad while I was away and was also very excited about starting his university education.

I left on my trip to see Mum, but it was only a short time before the demands came that I return. Before I left, I had been feeling surplus to what my role should be in Bob's family. However on this occasion, I was told it was my son who was not a happy camper. It was not working out — him living with Bob's family. I still to this day do not know what the problem was. Bob had called me, asking me to come home. Maybe my son wanted me to return, maybe it was Bob. I will never know. I just knew that I missed my son terribly and was more than happy to be back.

My son and I had moved into a small bungalow, just around the corner from the rest of the family. I was told it had been purchased in my son's name. Supposedly, my son had 97 per cent ownership and I had the remaining three per cent. I was delighted! Maybe all my years of devotion to Bob had not be in vain. My son would not only finish university with a degree and a new car, but he would also have his own home.

I was always the one to bring up the subject of his will. I knew Bob had a family trust, a financial instrument which I did not understand. I didn't want to let the issue drop — what if anything happened when Bob was away, where would that leave me and my son?

I believed Bob when he told me my son would be taken care of so I felt that going forward all would be well. At the same time, I was worried that my son might never be able to claim what was rightfully his because his birth certificate was incorrect. Bob's family member whom I had married was listed as the father on my son's birth certificate, not Bob.

Bob's response to any related discussions hurt me more than anything else. 'I provided my son with a university education,' he said. 'And I bought him his car ... also now his home. For an outside child, that's enough.'

Time was running out for me to try and put things right. My divorce from his nephew was now sorted out and it wouldn't be long before my son would turn eighteen. From the age of majority, he would be the one responsible for correcting his own birth certificate. He did not have a materialistic bone in his body and often said he did not care about such things. I felt my hands were tied as my pleas for his father to step up to the plate and correct this issue went unheard.

When my son turned 18, his brothers decided to take him to a strip joint. It was not their father's hotel, but it was one that Bob and I had frequented before. We knew the owner and it was not uncommon for us to hang out at each other's establishments.

My son still tells the story to this day of when he was taken to a strip club by his brothers and found his parents there.

Bob's desire for a threesome with his wife came up again and again, each time with renewed persistence. I don't know which one of us he worked on first or the most, or what was said to her. All I know is that one day, the three of us went for drinks and ended up in the same hotel room. His fantasy was playing out, and the driving factor that got us to that point was that it would be a special gift for his birthday.

After that threesome, he occasionally joked that going forward if he ever got caught sleeping with me, he would be able to say to his wife, 'Oh, so it's okay for you to sleep with her but not for me.' The wife either genuinely did not know that we were already sleeping together on a regular basis, or she chose to ignore it. I believe the latter to be the truth.

27

THE WEDDINGS

Bob's eldest son became quite successful over the years and had chosen a beautiful woman to marry. It was a joyous time. My son was part of their wedding party and when the wedding day arrived, he was seated at the head table along with his brothers. He gave a lovely speech to his brother and his new wife.

Obviously, it was a challenge for them to decide where to put me on such an occasion. I was placed well away from immediate family, among casual acquaintances of Bob's, like people who had done work for him over the years at the parlour. Of course, that did not sit well with me. Once again, I was silently hurt but what could I really expect them to do with me? My ability to put on a phony smile was more than severely challenged that day.

Years later, Bob's middle son who was being trained by his father to follow in his footsteps in the hotel business, had also chosen a stunning woman to marry. Their wedding was to take place at the lake house on what turned out to be a very hot day. My son had taken the necessary legal steps to be the person to officiate and join them in matrimony. He did a good job and spoke so eloquently. He has a good speaking voice and loves having a microphone in his hand, not to mention a captive audience. I beamed with pride just listening to him.

I had never felt comfortable mingling with unknown family members, so I stayed out of the way. At one point early in the evening, I found myself in the cottage chatting with Bob's grandchildren. We knelt on the couch looking out onto the lake. A storm was brewing due to the hot weather. Most of the guests were still outside in a large canopy tent. The kids and I were laughing and joking around when the eldest girl point blank asked me, 'You are not really your son's mum, are you?'

'What do you mean?' I asked, taken aback.

'You're not his real mum.'

I understood that kids will be kids and can be pretty blunt, but what was said that day must have come from a discussion about me with adults, most likely their parents. I explained the best I could. It was awkward for all of us.

As I looked out over the lake, I saw that the neighbour's helicopter had broken loose and was floating away. They had just recently purchased it and had it sitting on a floating, wooden pad attached to an extended dock. It was my opportunity to escape from the uncomfortable conversation with the children. I jumped up and ran out on the deck to call my son. He alerted his brothers, who jumped into the lake to chase down the floating helicopter.

Their saving the helicopter was all very exciting and they deserved the applause they got. The neighbour, however, who had been at the party all along, never did thank me for alerting everyone in the first place. I wonder where that helicopter would have ended up if I had not been sitting at that window.

I knew my son's brothers loved their mum very much and I never wanted them to hate me for being the other woman. They were older than my son, and were often out and about in the city and frequented the local bar scene. I never wanted them to know about Bob and me so I would refuse to go a lot of places Bob wanted me to go; I never wanted to bump into his kids anywhere. Being caught in the strip joint had really shook me up.

28

WHORE

Due to the fear I had of bumping into his children, Bob decided that the best way for the two of us to spend some quality time together was to rent a hotel room. We did that monthly, sometimes weekly, taking a couple of bottles of wine along and ordering in food. We treated the room like it was our private space for the day, leaving just in time to join the rest of the family for dinner at his home. I always wondered why those dinners with family never seemed to affect him in any way. After our day of intimacy, it seemed that it was me alone that suffered the culpability.

That uncomfortable situation seemed to get worse year by year, eventually causing me to pull away from family get togethers whenever I could. Bob wanted to be around his new grandbabies, which was perfectly understandable. The addition of grandchildren afforded me more freedom.

My son was totally absorbed with his brothers, his friends, and his studying. He was busy loving his life, singing, and acting in different plays.

As for me, something was happening that I did not understand for quite a while. When I finally did, I told Bob I was tired of my life as it was and that going into hotel rooms with him on a weekly basis made me feel like nothing more than a whore.

'That's because you are one,' he replied.

My brain almost exploded!

Of course, he tried to say he was joking. But it was that matter-of-fact way he had said it, so horribly mean, and with a glare to go with it. It hurt like hell because I was sure he meant it.

With age creeping up on me, I started to worry about all the what-ifs that could happen in my life. The big one was, what if something happened to Bob? How would my son and I manage without him? He often told me not to worry about those things. I said, 'But I do! You pay the mortgage and the taxes. What do I do if something happens to you?'

As age crept up on me, the more insecure I felt. I was now in my early sixties and had been in business for close to forty years. The distance between Bob and I had grown since his grandchildren had been born. I understood the love that Bob and his wife shared for them all, they were beautiful kids. I loved them too. Bob's usual demand for my time and attention was becoming less and less. My son was totally absorbed with his own adventures at university as he now belonged to a drama group. I wanted nothing more than to make sure that my son was part of what I helped build over the past forty years. But I had an awful feeling that it wouldn't be that way at all. I was right.

When Bob felt my son was old enough to understand, he told him the truth of how he was conceived. He had not been conceived through artificial insemination — that story was just for Bob's wife's ears, he told him. 'You were born the natural way.'

I realized that either story must have been difficult for my son to hear. I had always told him he was a miracle baby, much wanted and much loved. As time passed, I began to question things and see things for what they really were. Why did Bob behave the way he did and why did I put up with it? I started reading more, trying to educate myself. I felt there was something wrong with Bob and there must be a name for it.

I learned that Bob was a narcissist. He ticked off all the right boxes. I started to feel ashamed and sorry for his wife, realising that she was more affected than I. I began to see myself in a different light. Yes, I was the other woman but, on the positive side, that meant I was the fun, frivolous one, his righthand person at work, someone who was always there and totally reliable. At the same time, I would always be just the other woman — nothing more than a sex object and a home wrecker.

The person who was supposed to benefit from all the years of deception was my son. I grew to realize that he, too, was damaged because of our relationship with his father. He had grown up with his own defence mechanisms; he literally threw himself into his artistic ventures and kept a tightknit circle of friends. I care so deeply for my son, but I cannot go back and change things. My words will never be enough to show how sorry

I am for what I now understand as nothing more than my own selfish choices. My son has protected himself with a shell that, at times, even I find difficult to break through.

I will always love him. He always makes me proud to be his mum.

29

THERAPY

Mental health gets a lot of attention these days. It even seems to be all the rage to talk to a therapist. My therapy started in an unusual way and ended shockingly.

I believe I had a mental breakdown that day. I was at my doctor's office, picking up a prescription. I went to use the bathroom and it was busy so I took the elevator up to the next level. I had a hard time stopping my tears from falling that day as Bob's horrible words kept replaying in my mind. I could usually hold my tears back and put a smile on my face, but I was so unhappy I simply couldn't achieve that result.

I remember seeing a sign on a door that said 'Psychiatrist' along with the doctor's name. I walked in to an empty space and tried to open the next door which was directly in front of me, but the door was locked. I sat down in an adjoining room and looked around me. It was a beautiful space with easy listening music playing. I sat there and just cried and cried and cried. After almost an hour, the locked door opened and a well-dressed woman came out. She was saying goodbye to a patient. She then looked at me and said 'Can I help you?'

'Yes,' I said. 'I need someone to talk to, do you do that, are you the psychiatrist?'

She looked at me and said, 'It doesn't work like that. You have to make an appointment.'

I felt stupid and apologized. As I tried to pass by her to leave the room, but she stopped me by holding my arm.

'Go to your GP and tell her that I will see you if she sends a request.'

So that is exactly what I did. I went straight to my doctor's office and said, 'This lady psychiatrist, Dr. Lorne, said that she would see me if you filled out the form.' My doctor looked at me and said, 'I don't know how you accomplished this,' and gave me the form that I needed. I didn't have to wait long before I got the phone call to go in for my appointment.

After several meetings with her, only one thing stuck in my mind, and I never went back. In the last session I attended, referring to Bob, she asked me, 'Do you not think that this man was just trying to help you?'

I was shocked! I could not believe that after all I had told her that she could come up with such a question!

I went to England to see my mum. Her illness was so advanced, I didn't want to leave her. But I needed to go back to Canada and deal with my life.

When I returned, I stopped going to work and I told Bob that I wanted to retire. I was now sixty-two years old.

He, of course, made it all about the money. 'What will you live on?' he asked, as if he did not know my financial situation.

But I didn't care. He made me angry, talking about nothing but money at such a sad time in my life. I found myself in a deep dark hole of depression. My mum was close to death and there was nothing I could do. She no longer recognised any of her family and it was very hard. I had only been back in Canada for a couple of weeks and I knew I should never have left. I talked to my sister on the phone. She told me that Mum had continued to fail — her eyes were no longer focused and she was no longer eating.

Within 24 hours, Mum passed away. I was there for the funeral, but I did not get to say goodbye. I came back to Canada with the thought of never going back to work. Bob had showed me a nasty side of himself. After talking with my son, he convinced me to leave Bob and return to England permanently.

'You and Dad cannot live in the same country,' he told me. 'You should leave.' I agreed with my son. My son was over 18 now and finished his university with a masters in English and a major in Drama. I was very proud of him. He had no desire to live in England, but he thought I would be happier there.

Before I left, I wanted Bob to bring me the necessary papers so I could sign over my share of the house to my son.

The subsequent daily visits with Bob turned meaner as I found more and more inner strength to argue for what I wanted to do with my life.

Finally, he seemed to give in. 'Let's not part with all this anger between us,' he said, 'let me take you away.'

I was imprisoned by the kind of perverse loyalty that captures long-term, abused, women. Or else a big part of me still loved him. Either way, I was controlled by him, and I knew he would take advantage and probably spend any time away trying to change my mind about leaving once and for all.

I let him persuade me to go away with him as one last farewell, but I was secretly determined not to budge from my decision to leave. But my mind was made up. I was going home.

Bob and I arranged that I would meet up with him in his home country, then we would go on to his friend's oceanside cottage. That friend, Mr. Wealthy, had become a good friend since the infamous house party. Bob always travelled with a friend to cover his infidelities. This time was no different. When I arrived at the airport, I was greeted by Bob and his travelling companion. We went straight to a beautiful oceanside home that was one of Mr. Wealthy's properties.

Mr. Wealthy asked me why, of all things, had we decided to break up during a holiday. I explained that I had left work and I was retiring. I told him I might not see Bob ever again because I was returning home to England. 'Who knows what life has in store for any of us,' I said. 'My son will still visit me, and vice versa.' I told him I had asked my son to come back to England with me, but he had no intention of leaving the family and his friends.

'Well, if Bob doesn't look after you financially, you tell me,' he said. 'You have put a lot of years into his business and this relationship.'

This was all said in front of Bob. Not once did I throw him under the bus with the truth about my going home penniless after thirty-eight years of working alongside of him. I may have been the devoted mother of one of his sons, his business manager, his lover, his confidant, etc., etc., but at the end of the day, I was still just his 'outside' woman.

When we returned from that little farewell vacation, I was even more headstrong about doing what I had set out to do — which was to return to England.

Once I was back in the UK, my brother gave me a place to stay and let me live rent free. In turn, I helped wherever I could in his pub. It was good to keep busy. My management experience and skills were of value when my brother took off for weekly jaunts to Spain and Portugal.

Unfortunately, for Bob, things never really changed. Arguments continued between us, even though I was 3,000 miles away. I told him that it should never have ended up being my brother's responsibility to take care of me.

Then, things deteriorated at the pub. My brother had a long-term girlfriend who seemed to have taken control of him. Sometimes they didn't talk to each other for days at a time, which made for a terrible environment. I was out of place and felt very uncomfortable. I didn't seem to belong anywhere. My unease grew to the point that I felt that in every direction I went was only hostility.

To get away from the toxic environment at my brother's,

I went to my sister's and stayed for a while. But I soon knew that she and her hubby really did not want me there.

It was Christmas but I was not much fun. I broke down a lot with being separated from my son and my life … whatever that was.

Once again, I took to the air, not expecting that my return to my son would be accepted with much joy. I hadn't been gone that long. He was at his disc jockey job when I landed on New Year's Eve. I paid for the cab from the airport with my last $20.

It took Bob just a few days to show up at the door to tell me with his voice of authority that my life was the way it was because I just didn't listen to him. I think what he really meant was that I never fully accepted my lot as 'the outside woman.' 'No! My life is the way it is because I did listen.' I replied. 'I listened to you!'

Thoughts of that therapist went through my head, as they often had since I last saw her. She had also told me on one visit that she could give me a number for a legal-aid lawyer. 'You have rights,' she had said, 'even as a mistress, you have rights. You keep calling yourself a "mistress,"' she added, 'but in actual fact you were one of two wives, and everybody knew that.'

'*Everyone but me,*' I thought.

I had never pursued her suggestion to seek legal aid. I always felt that financial support should have been offered to me with kindness from the person to whom I had given almost 40 years of my life.

As much as my son was pleased to see me, he made it known that he did not want to be a 30-year-old guy still living with his mum. He offered to sell the house and buy each of us a smaller home. I told him not to worry, that I really wasn't going to be around that long. Once more, I painted on a smile and said I totally understood. But considering what I was going through mentally, his new desire for independence could not have come at a worse time. I said I was just there to tie up loose ends, close bank accounts, and get the papers signed for the mortgage transfer to him.

Bob asked me if I wanted to meet for dinner and talk. Again, I thought it best to part on friendly terms, if possible, primarily for my son's benefit, so we met. I explained to Bob that I was going to give my tenants who were living in my mother's home three months' notice and then sell the house. I could never live in it myself because it held too many childhood memories.

I asked him how long he thought the paperwork would take for me to sign the local house over to my son.

'Probably next week,' he said.

The conversation then progressed to how he was training and dating a new desk person and manager.

'Yes,' I responded. 'I've heard … and I think it's all too disgusting … you're dating a woman half your age. At least when we got together, I wasn't with you for the money. I helped you make it to the top of your game.' I told him that surely it could not make him feel good knowing that the young girl was with him just for the money. 'Don't you find it at all a bit embarrassing?' I asked. I enjoyed getting my little digs in where and when I could and the arguing continued.

He tried to convince me to stay and offered me a deal that involved my taking over his role in the business because he was aging and felt ready to take a back seat. The offer would have been enticing if not for the control he would have over me, control I had fought so hard to get away from. He said it would be different because he just wanted to spend more time with his grandkids, but I didn't believe him.

He said it would just entail my going into the office for a couple of hours each day and doing the books and banking, and generally keeping an eye on the staff by phone during the open hours. Along with that offer, I would be expected to take all the paperwork around to him at his home, every day, if not every second day.

I had accepted the dinner invitation with the sole purpose of having us both get things off our chests without shouting at each other. That didn't happen. But being forever the optimist, I thought at least we were talking to each other.

Bob brought the paperwork around to the house later that week and said, 'Sign here, and print your name there.' But this time I read it first thoroughly. To my shock and utter dismay, it stated that the house had never been primarily my son's. Instead, the original ownership had been split four ways between Bob, his wife, myself, and my son. I was being asked to sign my share over to Bob, his wife, and my son.

I told him I was not removing my name from the original document and four-way split. He claimed he did not know it had been written up like that in the first place, which would have been years before. I didn't believe him for a second and called him a liar.

'Why would you, for the longest time, let my son and I think the house was his?' I asked and then told him to leave. 'And don't come back while I am still here,' I said.

'There you go again,' he shouted on his way out, 'wasting my fucking money on lawyers.'

After my son and I talked it over, he agreed we should just leave all the paperwork as it is.

30

FREEDOM

I had made the trip overseas dozens of times since first leaving England when I was 19 and felt like I had the whole world at my fingertips. Most of those trips were good holiday breaks and family time – but many were attempts to escape whatever disaster I was making of my life at the moment. But I had never, ever felt so alone returning to England as I did after that meeting with Bob to sign the house papers. I knew that I had to make things work for myself if I was truly to be totally independent.

I was leaving with huge credit card bills, along with a line of credit over $20,000. Most of it had accumulated from the cost of travelling back and forth when my mum was ill and dying. Ordinarily, I would have paid a huge chunk of those bills off with my $20,000 Christmas bonus, but, of course, I never got paid that bonus cheque because I left.

Although I had always tried to buy good appliances and furniture, thinking it would benefit my son in the future, I knew I was not good with money. I had always been looked after by a man, first by my husband Richard, and then by Bob. But I knew I had to get my head around finances and living an independent life. It would be extremely hard for me. I knew that. But the hardest thing I ever had to do was leave my son. That last time, I left to fly home , it felt so permanent.

I tried to convince my son to take counselling himself. I knew I was not the only one who had been damaged by all the drama. I had left my son in the clutches of his dad's control ... the very place I had finally escaped. But he convinced me that he would be okay, and so I left. I wore sunglasses for most of the long trip home because my thoughts kept wandering back, and tears would fall uncontrollably.

Upon arrival in England, I went directly to my mother's home. It was empty, damp, and full of mould – disgusting! My tenants had left within the first month of the three-month notice I had given them which further added to my financial woes. For some reason, I had trusted them to leave at the very end of the three-month notice. How naive I had been.

Along with the emotional weight of having left my son, I had to figure out how to live on my government pension of just $700 a month. It was used up just making minimum payments on loans and credit cards. I was in a deep, financial mess.

I had to stay in the house, but I refused to sleep upstairs. Not only was there the mold to deal with, I felt afraid, scared.

It was not just the spiders that used to crawl in under the patio doors each night, sad memories lived everywhere in that house. I borrowed a blow up bed from my brother-in-law and settled in on the main floor.

It was the first time I had lived by myself since I was 19. After the breakup of my first marriage, I had roommates, lovers, and then, or course, the joyful company of my son.

I put the house up for sale straight away.

After a couple of weeks alone, my pub-running brother broke up with his long-term partner and, luckily for me, he came to my house to stay, bringing along my mum's little dog that he had promised to take care of when she died. We had both been unsuccessful in our relationships and often spoke of the sorry mess we found ourselves in.

I felt sure the house would soon sell, even though I had not had any viewers. Again, always the naïve optimist.

Luckily, I had brought my iPad with me, which enabled me to help my brother register for government housing. To add to his woes, he had spent the last several months recovering from prostate cancer.

We found a place he liked. A friend and I helped him scrub it all down, paint, and decorate. It turned out lovely and in just four months he was in it.

No one was coming to see my mum's house and my financial situation was getting worse and worse. I had to suck up my pride and ask my brother-in-law for help. He said he would loan me £1000, even more if I wanted it, and I could pay him back when the house sold.

I had purchased a new mattress with the last bit of room

on my credit card. I was getting quite desperate when, at last, the real estate agent phoned and told me he had someone to view the house. I was desperate to sell because of my debt load and accepted his first offer – £20,000 (about $40,000 Canadian) under the asking price. My agent asked me, 'Do you not want to counter the offer?'

I said, 'No, I don't want to lose the buyer. I accept.'

I knew the money would eventually come to me, but it was taking forever. I called my aunt in Canada to ask her to loan me $10,000 until the house deal went through and thankfully, she sent the money to me straight away. When the money from the house finally came, I paid off all my debts, almost $50,000, which felt wonderful. I vowed never to get in debt to that degree again.

My sister talked me into buying a one-bed flat as opposed to renting somewhere. It made sense to me. All I could afford was a very small flat, but it was very cosy and I fell in love with it.

31

SURPRISE

If I was to stay out of debt, I would need a job. However, rumours had started going round about where I had previously worked. Because I was there to live among the community instead of just for the usual short stint, people were more curious about me than if I was just a visitor.

However, upon getting the keys to my little flat, I was greeted by a pile of human faeces on my doormat. And, to my disgust, I had not noticed it until I had tracked it throughout the kitchen. My brother, who was helping me move, was in as much shock as I was. I broke down. I could not believe people could be so mean.

Someone had previously approached me in the pub and said, 'Oh, so you're the madam that everyone is talking about.'

Because of that, I felt for sure that the doorstep incident was related to my former occupation.

In the privacy of my home, I was, once again, a mess. But I had had a lot of years of experience painting my smile on before going out to face the world.

The word *brothel*, which was the term used in England, seemed so much harsher than *massage parlour*. Just hearing the word disgusted me. I was trying desperately to be done with that life, but it refused to be done with me. I truly wanted to defend myself, saying that where I worked was a luxurious establishment not a dive — but I kept my mouth shut, hoping that all the gossip would go away on its own.

I moved into the flat on the first of October and, as much as I enjoyed furnishing the place with new things, I found myself in tears every day. I missed my son so much.

As the Christmas season approached, a friend convinced me to walk with her for an hour every day to cheer me up, but it did not work. I just cried and told her I was not doing Christmas. It just did not feel like the holiday season to me. And, true to my word, I never bought gifts or cards. I was in a mess with all that I had been through and I was trying hard to move on from leaving my son alone so far away.

For some reason, everyone in my family gathered at my place. It was Christmas whether I wanted it or not, and they were all stepping up in any way they could to help me set up my new home.

In the midst of all the activity, my doorbell rang unexpectedly. When no one responded after my second request for someone to answer it, I made my way to do it myself. I opened the door to find someone standing there all wrapped up in Christmas paper. I was not particularly amused, but someone was trying to be funny, so I co-operated. I stood back for a second before moving forward to rip off the paper.

To my utter shock, under all that wrapping stood my son! It was the greatest gift of my entire miserable life!

I screamed with delight. I cried, I hugged, and I cried some more. I could not believe it. Every one of my family members had known about the surprise for a month. How they kept it a secret when I was so downtrodden is still beyond me. I could not believe that even my close friend had kept it from me during our daily walks, especially when I had regularly cried and told her over and over how much I missed him.

He could stay to visit for just four days, but it was the best four days ever. The blow-up bed was brought back into service in the kitchen. The place was cramped but, oh how I loved it.

After everyone had left, I poured my heart out to him about how broke I was and how I had borrowed money left and right. I even told him about the nasty present I had found on the doorstep when I moved in, and how people were being ugly toward me because of my previous work. He encouraged me to register a complaint with the police in case it became a bigger issue.

He told me that Bob had paid for his trip to see me. I said I was thankful for that.

Then, he told me he was thinking of seeing a psychiatrist … at a $100 an hour. I told him to go through his personal doctor because that way his therapy fee would be paid by Medicare. But whatever choice he made, it would be good for him to talk to someone. His disclosure confirmed in my mind what I had long suspected. He was struggling as much as I was with the changes over the previous years. As a mother, I felt helpless to support him in his time of need.

We went to my sister's place for Christmas dinner and then to one of her renowned parties on Boxing Day. My son put a video up on their large screen TV of a song from one of his recent CDs. He had always loved to sing so Bob was apparently building him a recording room in the basement of my son's home. He sang along with the CD, and everyone thought he was brilliant. One young woman came forward and asked him to sign her chest. He seemed to be embarrassed by that kind of attention, but for the rest of us, the ask was quite hilarious.

Later, he asked me if I would do a podcast with him about my life and, in turn, he was going to ask his dad to do one as well. 'No!' I told him without hesitation. Too many people would get hurt and, besides, his dad would never tell the truth. I also told him that Bob had lied every single day of his life, and not just to me.

After the Boxing Day party, we walked back to my little flat together, about a mile down the road. He told me never to walk that same route alone again, especially since the faeces incident. The route went through an open field and down dark snickets.

It was so nice to feel the reversal of caring roles between us. He made me proud to know that I had instilled such values in him over the years.

When we reached my flat, we looked through photos while waiting for the early morning taxi that would take him away from me and off to the airport. He put money in my hand and then, in the blink of an eye, he was gone.

I talked to him several times throughout his journey, then I was alone again. I thought things were improving for me a little after getting through the holidays, but one day, due to my increase in walking, I acquired plantar fasciitis. Later, I slipped in the shower and cut my leg. I had to have the dressing on my leg changed every second day because the wound had ulcerated.

To add to my dismay, I came home one day to find another big pile of faeces on my doorstep. When I talked to my son, he convinced me to report it, especially since it was not just a one-time thing. I told the police that I wanted the incident on record. They said they would send someone round to take a report, but I said, 'No, I don't want that. I just want it on record that I have spoken to you.'

32

CHANGE OF PLAN
- COVID 19

Early in February following my son's Christmas surprise visit, I got a panicked call from him. Bob had been rushed to hospital and the family had been called to say their last goodbyes. I was in total shock! I felt helpless. Text after text burned through cyberspace.

To everyone's relief, including mine, Bob somehow came through that episode but was diagnosed with a fatal lung disease. There was no cure. His lungs had lost all elasticity, which could prevent him from breathing if he went into a coughing spell. It could take his life at any time.

After a few more days in the hospital, he was released, given a portable oxygen tank and told there was nothing anyone could do to change the death sentence he had been given.

Before my son left England, he had told me his dad was taking the whole family on a week's vacation to Mexico. I thought that was nice. However, because of Bob taking ill, the trip was cancelled.

I was sad for him. What he had I would not wish on anyone, not even my worst enemy. I decided to text him and tell him that I loved him and that it was sad after so many years of loving and caring about each other that we had separated on such awful terms. If we could have seen into the future, maybe things said between us would not have been said so harshly. I told him I was genuinely sorry for what he was going through.

Other phone calls were never about me returning to him. We both knew we had gone too far for that. I felt the coldness on the phone while he let me speak. I knew him well enough that because I had walked out of his life, he had programmed his mind not to care even one little bit about me. People like him are not forgiving. Period! No empathy.

He paid for private medication, which was very expensive, and a special breathing machine installed at his home. The portable oxygen tank was mainly used to enable him to drive, continuing to take care of his business affairs from the comfort of his new Porsche.

But he was losing weight drastically and, as each day passed, he found it more and more difficult to talk. I told my son that if anything should happen, I would return for the funeral to support him.

Then, toward the end of February 2020, Covid 19 hit England hard. Lives were lost and people were ordered by governments to stay inside and not mingle. Everyone was to wear masks to protect others and themselves. Many businesses closed. Everyone suffered greatly.

I had often told my son that I would like to live six months in England and return to Canada for the summer months. When the time came that I was unable to travel, then maybe he would regularly come to England to see me. But with the added threat of Covid 19, and as I had done all of my life, I began to second guess — what if I never got to see him again at all?

With the added risk of catching Covid, I feared the outside world more than ever. During that time, I had my food delivered and never left the flat. And as one might expect, I descended into depression again.

I knew things were not great for my son financially; he told me he had taken in a friend as a roommate to share expenses. He was losing people he knew to Covid, and I was on the wrong side of the ocean to give him any true support. I vowed that if I got out of the Covid thing alive I would sell my flat and return to him, and never leave him by himself again.

Meanwhile, Bob had taken to calling me on a regular basis. He was still very ill but whenever he drove out to the lake, he would call me and tell me about what he was doing for our son. Naturally, that made me happy. Sometimes the calls would turn into serious discussions, but I didn't tell him what was really on my mind. I was afraid to — I knew each conversation could be our last.

Most people become humble and grateful near the end, or so I always believed. But not Bob. He still said things to try to hurt me, and was disrespectful whenever he could. He told me how difficult it was for everyone financially with his illness and how Covid was affecting business and commerce everywhere. He always mentioned how he continued to go out of his way to help our son.

On one of those phone calls, I broached the subject of putting my son's birth certificate right.

'It's just a piece of paper,' he replied sharply. 'My son doesn't care about that … he knows I'm his dad.'

'Most fathers would want to claim birth rights to their children and would not want to just leave it hanging,' I said.

'All I care about is my grandkids,' he said. 'Everyone else has had opportunities, and as for those who didn't grasp them … well, that's not my responsibility.'

That remark was pointed directly at me. He threw it at me that our son never tried anything in the business world because I had always let him do whatever he wanted. It was my fault that he never learned business values, and that I let him believe the arts world was the right road for him.

The conversation was getting out of hand, so I left it by saying, 'You have changed your vocabulary from me being a girlfriend to being an outside woman. Please don't let your son feel like an outside child.'

'I blame you and your wife for taking him away from me,' I added. 'Now don't exclude him at the end by not giving him what his birthright entitles him to.' It was not long after that, that Bob's trips to the lake slowed down. Or he became the passenger when he could no longer drive out to the lake.

Sometimes he would call when he was waiting for his wife to come out of the grocery store. I would never cut him off, but I stopped giving strong opinions on certain issues that I knew would upset him. I would just listen to the day-to-day hardships that he was experiencing. I had a deep sense that things were coming to an end. Despite everything that had happened over the years and how he had treated me and our son, that made me very sad.

Finally, my flat in England sold, and travel restrictions were lifted, and I was able to book my ticket. A family member that I loved like my own had recently broken up after a long-term relationship of 20-plus years. She was waiting to get into her own home, and I told her that I would put all my new furniture that I had purchased in storage for her until she was ready to move. She was over the moon and thanked me to no end.

I started to get excited about my new life that lay ahead of me. I was leaving my family in England, all of whom had been fabulous. But they had their own little circles of family and friends. I was alone. I think my eldest brother, who had gone through two divorces and the loss of one of his children, was one of the few who truly knew the kind of loneliness I was experiencing.

33

BACK TO MY HAPPY
PLACE WITH MY SON

I was truly excited to see my son but felt very nervous about seeing Bob once again. My son picked me up at the airport and I couldn't wait to get back to our home where I had felt a sense of belonging and love from my son.

I felt responsible for the position my son was in. He could not just up and leave like a lot of young men do; he had the responsibility of the house. Even though he had been the one to encourage me to leave, I felt guilty because he was also left with the remnants of my bad choices. His dad still had full control over him, giving orders and expecting them to be followed – all based on the fact that Bob paid the mortgage and taxes.

The morning after I got back, Bob drove his car onto the driveway and called to ask our son to open the garage door so he could drive in, just as he had always done, except it was his son that he communicated with instead of me. That felt a little weird for some reason.

I thought I should go out and at least say hello, which I did. But it was like talking to a stranger ... very polite — and ice cold.

I could see he had lost a lot of weight and, with chronic shortness of breath, was having great difficulty talking. He must have felt a little awkward in front of me. He had always been such a strong 'boss man' character in my life.

I looked at him intently and started to break down as he continued to give my son orders about picking up supplies for the office and making a bank deposit. I couldn't speak. It was hard to see the man I had loved for years in such a state of decline. I picked up on the coldness of his demeanour and left them to finish talking.

I wondered, *Can you love and hate the same person at the same time?* I suppose it is possible, the same way it's possible for a man to love two women at the same time.

My son had been in communication with me prior to my leaving England and secured an apartment for me. I had put down a damage deposit, but I knew I would not be able to keep it long as it was too expensive. He helped me get sorted out, setting up my bed, and I soon felt settled. My dominant thought was, *'Surely now my life can only change for the better.'*

34

LOSING THE ONES
YOU LOVE

A week went by. Bob was deteriorating fast. Then, just two weeks after my return, I got a phone call from my sister in England. My beloved niece, who I loved like my own, had fallen down some stairs and was on life support. Memories automatically flashed through my mind of the times we had spent together over the years, including the time she lived here in Canada along with my sister and her husband. She was just two years old, and was such a joy.

More traumatic phone calls went back and forth. She was not going to make it. Within hours of the original call, she was gone.

I was physically sick. I couldn't sleep. Ordinarily, I would have taken the first flight back home, but what if my son's father also died while I was on the other side of the Atlantic? I had to remind myself that the journey home was not as simple as catching a bus. I could easily get to the other side of the Atlantic to help console my sister but then not make it back if Bob passed away.

I don't know if anyone can really explain grief. Words are not enough. I was confused about what my role should be. Should I be at my sister's side when I had just spent months crying to be at my son's side?

I decided my role was to be with my son , even though it was almost two years since I had left him to move permanently back to England. I felt that the apron strings had been well and truly cut. A grown man stood in front of me where my little boy used to be. As a man, he stepped up for me, organizing so many things through the transition into my new apartment. Once again, he made me so very proud of him.

He announced one day that during the Covid lockdown he had been talking online with a young woman. He had become quite fond of her, and I could not wait to meet her. He seemed to be love-struck. I knew there had been a huge change in him. He did not need me as much anymore, but I needed him more than ever. Our roles had reversed.

I invited the two of them for supper and could see why he was so in love with her. She was a breath of fresh air. It was a joy to watch them together.

I had not spoken to Bob for quite a while. He had become housebound, unable even to get around in his vehicle. Part of me wanted to visit him at home but I was scared that I would be received with the same coldness that I got when Bob had come to my son's house. Aside from that, I knew I wouldn't be able to hold it together emotionally — or even speak. And maybe the wife would finally tell me to go away.

As few days passed and my son called me, giving me the sad news of his dad's passing. I quickly drove to my son's house. He had already left to go to his father's house to join his brothers.

In and out of crying, I tried to make myself useful at my son's by tidying up. I felt so helpless. I could not go over to Bob's house. I hadn't spoken to the family for the longest time. I curled up on the couch and waited for my son to return. When he did come back, I could see he was upset. Of course, he was upset! I gave him a hug and consoled him as best I could, but I sensed he wanted to be alone, so I left.

A few days later he came to my apartment with his girlfriend with news that was difficult for him to deliver. It was a bombshell – the wife did not want me at Bob's funeral! I cried, 'Who gets barred from attending a funeral?' Was it even a sincere statement, or did it just come from a petty need for revenge? I did not know, and never will. My son cried when he gave me this news as he knew it would be hurtful.

Since Bob's passing, I have slowly been building my relationship with my son.

Thankfully, my life has finally moved beyond all the drama. I have made good strides toward getting the love of my son back into my life, which is all that really matters.

I regularly reread the letter that I still have from my dad when he was in his sober days. He was trying to convince me to return home and get away from the path of sin that I was stuck on. He had warned me about the loneliness that he foresaw in my future. I just never had the strength of character to listen, let alone take his advice.

When I go into my memory box, I also read Bob's letters that he sent me professing his undying love. I fervently wish I had been strong enough to leave all those long years ago.

I know my son was damaged by my relationship with his father. I am not proud of many things, but I am proud of my son. He has grown up with his own defence mechanism. He literally throws himself into his artistic ventures. I am blessed with the fact that he has a good heart and a caring attitude toward people. He is not at all materialistic and drives around in a ten-year-old car with high mileage. I promised my share of the home to my son the day I left it. He knows that my word is good.

I love him with all my heart. He is the reason I breathe. The way he was born was selfish in the extreme, but he was born, and since that moment, I have been a devoted mother.

Now at seventy years of age, I am a happy senior, living in a 55-plus building in a space of 750 square feet. I receive rent assistance to help make it through from one month to the next. I volunteer in a food kitchen that feeds the elderly, a task that keeps me out of trouble, as they say. I am happy that my son and his beautiful girlfriend are in my life. I am patiently waiting for grandkids. My son says that is not in the cards ... but accidents happen!

ACKNOWLEDGEMENTS

My heartfelt thanks goes to my son for supporting
me and giving me the strength and brazenness to go
to print with this very personal book. Your support,
lending an ear to my life — a life misunderstood in
so many ways is more special than anything else.

Special appreciation goes to my family for not judging me and
my life of bad choices. I am so grateful — especially to those
closest family members who gave me generous encouragement
along the way to get my story into the public realm.

I would also like to thank my closest of friends,
who convinced me that I had led a different life
than most and that my story should be told.

www.ingramcontent.com/pod-product-compliance
Lightning Source LLC
Chambersburg PA
CBHW062131020426
42335CB00013B/1181